Also by Andrew Bacevich

The Long War:
A New History of U.S. National Security Policy
Since World War II

The New American Militarism:
How Americans Are Seduced by War

American Empire:
The Realities and Consequences of U.S. Diplomacy

The Imperial Tense:
Prospects and Problems of American Empire

THE LIMITS OF POWER

The End of American Exceptionalism

Andrew J. Bacevich

Metropolitan Books
Henry Holt and Company
New York

Set thine house in order.

—2 Kings, chapter 20, verse 1

Holt Paperbacks
Henry Holt and Company, LLC
Publishers since 1866
175 Fifth Avenue
New York, New York 10010
www.henryholt.com

Library of Congress Cataloging-in-Publication data

Bacevich, A. J.
    The limits of power / Andrew J. Bacevich.—1st ed.
        p. cm.
    Includes bibliographical references and index.
    ISBN-13: 978-0-8050-9016-1
    ISBN-10: 0-8050-9016-9
    1. United States—Politics and government—1993–2001.
    2. United States—Politics and government—2001–   3. Power
(Social sciences)—United States.   I. Title.
    JK271.B24 2008
    320.973—dc22   2008007040

Henry Holt books are available for special promotions and premiums.
For details contact: Director, Special Markets.

Originally published in hardcover in 2008 by Metropolitan Books
First Holt Paperbacks Edition 2009
Designed by Meryl Sussman Levavi

Printed in the United States of America
1 3 5 7 9 10 8 6 4 2

To the memory of my beloved son

ANDREW JOHN BACEVICH

First Lieutenant, U.S. Army

July 8, 1979–May 13, 2007

Contents

Introduction:
War Without Exits

For the United States, the passing of the Cold War yielded neither a "peace dividend" nor anything remotely resembling peace. Instead, what was hailed as a historic victory gave way almost immediately to renewed unrest and conflict. By the time the East-West standoff that some historians had termed the "Long Peace" ended in 1991, the United States had already embarked upon a decade of unprecedented interventionism.[1] In the years that followed, Americans became inured to reports of U.S. forces going into action—fighting in Panama and the Persian Gulf, occupying Bosnia and Haiti, lambasting Kosovo, Afghanistan, and Sudan from the air. Yet all of these turned out to be mere preliminaries. In 2001 came the main event, an open-ended global war on terror, soon known in some quarters as the "Long War."[2]

Viewed in retrospect, indications that the Long Peace began almost immediately to give way to conditions antithetical to peace seem blindingly obvious. Prior to 9/11, however, the implications of developments like the 1993 bombing of the World Trade Center or the failure of the U.S. military mission to Somalia that same year were difficult to discern. After all, these small events left unaltered what many took to be the defining reality of the contemporary era: the preeminence of the United States, which seemed beyond challenge.

During the 1990s, at the urging of politicians and pundits, Americans became accustomed to thinking of their country as "the indispensable nation." Indispensability carried with it both responsibilities and prerogatives.

The chief responsibility was to preside over a grand project of political-economic convergence and integration commonly referred to as globalization. In point of fact, however, globalization served as a euphemism for soft, or informal, empire. The collapse of the Soviet Union appeared to offer an opportunity to expand and perpetuate that empire, creating something akin to a global Pax Americana.

The indispensable nation's chief prerogative, self-assigned, was to establish and enforce the norms governing the post–Cold War international order. Even in the best of circumstances, imperial policing is a demanding task, requiring not only considerable acumen but also an abundance of determination. The preferred American approach was to rely, whenever possible, on suasion. Yet if pressed, Washington did not hesitate to use force, as its numerous military adventures during the 1990s demonstrated.

Whatever means were employed, the management of empire assumed the existence of bountiful reserves of power—economic, political, cultural, but above all military. In the immediate aftermath of the Cold War, few questioned that assumption.[3] The status of the United States as "sole superpower" appeared unassailable. Its dominance was unquestioned and unambiguous. This was not hypernational-istic chest-thumping; it was the conventional wisdom.

Recalling how Washington saw the post–Cold War world and America's place in (or atop) it helps us understand why policy makers failed to anticipate, deter, or deflect the ter-rorist attacks of September 11, 2001. A political elite preoccu-pied with the governance of empire paid little attention to protecting the United States itself. In practical terms, prior to 9/11 the mission of homeland defense was unassigned.

The institution nominally referred to as the Department of Defense didn't actually do defense; it specialized in power projection. In 2001, the Pentagon was prepared for any number of contingencies in the Balkans or Northeast Asia or the Persian Gulf. It was just not prepared to address threats to the nation's eastern seaboard. Well-trained and equipped U.S. forces stood ready to defend Seoul or Riyadh; Manhattan was left to fend for itself.

Odd as they may seem, these priorities reflected a core principle of national security policy: When it came to de-fending vital American interests, asserting control over the imperial periphery took precedence over guarding the na-tion's own perimeter.

After 9/11, the Bush administration affirmed this core principle. Although it cobbled together a new agency to at-tend to "homeland security," the administration also redou-bled its efforts to shore up the Pax Americana and charged the Department of Defense with focusing on this task. This meant using any means necessary—suasion where possible, force as required—to bring the Islamic world into conform-ity with prescribed American norms. Rather than soft and consensual, the approach to imperial governance became harder and more coercive.

So, for the United States after 9/11, war became a

seemingly permanent condition. President George W. Bush and members of his administration outlined a campaign against terror that they suggested might last decades, if not longer. On the national political scene, few questioned that prospect. In the Pentagon, senior military officers spoke in terms of "generational war," lasting up to a century.[4] Just two weeks after 9/11, Secretary of Defense Donald Rumsfeld was already instructing Americans to "forget about 'exit strategies'; we're looking at a sustained engagement that carries no deadlines."[5]

By and large, Americans were slow to grasp the implications of a global war with no exits and no deadlines. To earlier generations, place names like Iraq and Afghanistan had been synonymous with European rashness—the sort of obscure and unwelcoming jurisdictions to which overly ambitious kings and slightly mad adventurers might repair to squabble. For the present generation, it has already become part of the natural order of things that GIs should be exerting themselves at great cost to pacify such far-off domains. For the average American tuning in to the nightly news, reports of U.S. casualties incurred in distant lands now seem hardly more out of the ordinary than reports of partisan shenanigans on Capitol Hill or brush fires raging out of control in Southern California.

How exactly did the end of the Long Peace so quickly yield the Long War? Seeing themselves as a peaceful people, Americans remain wedded to the conviction that the conflicts in which they find themselves embroiled are not of their own making. The global war on terror is no exception. Certain of our own benign intentions, we reflexively assign responsibility for war to others, typically malignant Hitler-like figures inexplicably bent on denying us the peace that is our fondest wish.

This book challenges that supposition. It argues that the actions of Saddam Hussein and Osama bin Laden, however malevolent, cannot explain why the United States today finds itself enmeshed in seemingly never-ending conflict. Although critics of U.S. foreign policy, and especially of the Iraq War, have already advanced a variety of alternative explanations—variously fingering President Bush, members of his inner circle, jingoistic neoconservatives, greedy oil executives, or even the Israel lobby—it also finds those explanations inadequate. Certainly, the president and his advisers, along with neocons always looking for opportunities to flex American military muscle, bear considerable culpability for our current predicament. Yet to charge them with primary responsibility is to credit them with undeserved historical significance. It's the equivalent of blaming Herbert Hoover for the Great Depression or of attributing McCarthyism entirely to the antics of Senator Joseph McCarthy.

The impulses that have landed us in a war of no exits and no deadlines come from within. Foreign policy has, for decades, provided an outward manifestation of American domestic ambitions, urges, and fears. In our own time, it has increasingly become an expression of domestic dysfunction—an attempt to manage or defer coming to terms with contradictions besetting the American way of life. Those contradictions have found their ultimate expression in the perpetual state of war afflicting the United States today.

Gauging their implications requires that we acknowledge their source: They reflect the accumulated detritus of freedom, the by-products of our frantic pursuit of life, liberty, and happiness.

Freedom is the altar at which Americans worship, whatever their nominal religious persuasion. "No one sings odes to liberty as the final end of life with greater fervor than

Americans," the theologian Reinhold Niebuhr once observed.[6] Yet even as they celebrate freedom, Americans ex-
empt the object of their veneration from critical examination.
In our public discourse, freedom is not so much a word or
even a value as an incantation, its very mention enough to
stifle doubt and terminate all debate.

The Limits of Power will suggest that this heedless worship of freedom has been a mixed blessing. In our pursuit of
freedom, we have accrued obligations and piled up debts
that we are increasingly hard-pressed to meet. Especially
since the 1960s, freedom itself has undercut the nation's
ability to fulfill its commitments. We teeter on the edge of
insolvency, desperately trying to balance accounts by relying on our presumably invincible armed forces. Yet there,
too, having exaggerated our military might, we court bankruptcy.

The United States today finds itself threatened by three
interlocking crises. The first of these crises is economic and
cultural, the second political, and the third military. All
three share this characteristic: They are of our own making.
In assessing the predicament that results from these crises,
The Limits of Power employs what might be called a
Niebuhrean perspective. Writing decades ago, Reinhold
Niebuhr anticipated that predicament with uncanny accuracy and astonishing prescience. As such, perhaps more
than any other figure in our recent history, he may help us
discern a way out.

As pastor, teacher, activist, theologian, and prolific author, Niebuhr was a towering presence in American intellectual life from the 1930s through the 1960s. Even today, he
deserves recognition as the most clear-eyed of American
prophets. Niebuhr speaks to us from the past, offering
truths of enormous relevance to the present. As prophet, he

warned that what he called "our dreams of managing history"—born of a peculiar combination of arrogance and narcissism—posed a potentially mortal threat to the United States.[7] Today, we ignore that warning at our peril.

Niebuhr entertained few illusions about the nature of man, the possibilities of politics, or the pliability of history. Global economic crisis, total war, genocide, totalitarianism, and nuclear arsenals capable of destroying civilization itself—he viewed all of these with an unblinking eye that allowed no room for hypocrisy, hokum, or self-deception. Realism and humility formed the core of his worldview, each infused with a deeply felt Christian sensibility.

Realism in this sense implies an obligation to see the world as it actually is, not as we might like it to be. The enemy of realism is hubris, which in Niebuhr's day, and in our own, finds expression in an outsized confidence in the efficacy of American power as an instrument to reshape the global order.

Humility imposes an obligation of a different sort. It summons Americans to see themselves without blinders. The enemy of humility is sanctimony, which gives rise to the conviction that American values and beliefs are universal and that the nation itself serves providentially assigned purposes. This conviction finds expression in a determination to remake the world in what we imagine to be America's image.

In our own day, realism and humility have proven in short supply. What Niebuhr wrote after World War II proved truer still in the immediate aftermath of the Cold War: Good fortune and a position of apparent preeminence placed the United States "under the most grievous temptations to self-adulation."[8] Americans have given themselves over to those temptations. Hubris and sanctimony have become the paramount expressions of American statecraft.

After 9/11, they combined to produce the Bush administration's war of no exits and no deadlines.

President Bush has likened today's war against what he calls "Islamofascism" to America's war with Nazi Germany—a great struggle waged on behalf of liberty. That President Bush is waging his global war on terror to preserve American freedom is no doubt the case. Yet that commitment, however well intentioned, begs several larger questions: As actually expressed and experienced, what is freedom today? What is its content? What costs does the exercise of freedom impose? Who pays?

These are fundamental questions, which cannot be dismissed with a rhetorical wave of the hand. Great wartime presidents of the past—one thinks especially of Abraham Lincoln speaking at Gettysburg—have not hesitated to confront such questions directly. That President Bush seems oblivious to their very existence offers one measure of his shortcomings as a statesman.

Freedom is not static, nor is it necessarily benign. In practice, freedom constantly evolves and in doing so generates new requirements and abolishes old constraints. The common understanding of freedom that prevailed in December 1941 when the United States entered the war against Imperial Japan and Nazi Germany has long since become obsolete. In some respects, this must be cause for celebration. In others, it might be cause for regret.

The changes have been both qualitative and quantitative. In many respects, Americans are freer today than ever before, with more citizens than ever before enjoying unencumbered access to the promise of American life. Yet especially since the 1960s, the reinterpretation of freedom has had a transformative impact on our society and culture. That transformation has produced a paradoxical legacy. As individuals, our appetites and expectations have grown exponentially. Niebuhr once wrote disapprovingly of Americans, their "culture soft and vulgar, equating joy with happiness and happiness with comfort."[9] Were he alive today, Niebuhr might amend that judgment, with Americans increasingly equating comfort with self-indulgence.

The collective capacity of our domestic political economy to satisfy those appetites has not kept pace with demand. As a result, sustaining our pursuit of life, liberty, and happiness at home requires increasingly that Americans look beyond our borders. Whether the issue at hand is oil, credit, or the availability of cheap consumer goods, we expect the world to accommodate the American way of life.

The resulting sense of entitlement has great implications for foreign policy. Simply put, as the American appetite for freedom has grown, so too has our penchant for empire. The connection between these two tendencies is a causal one. In an earlier age, Americans saw empire as the antithesis of freedom. Today, as illustrated above all by the Bush administration's efforts to dominate the energy-rich Persian Gulf, empire has seemingly become a prerequisite of freedom.

There is a further paradox: The actual exercise of American freedom is no longer conducive to generating the power required to establish and maintain an imperial order. If anything, the reverse is true: Centered on consumption and individual autonomy, the exercise of freedom is contributing to the gradual erosion of our national power. At precisely the moment when the ability to wield power—especially military power—has become the sine qua non for preserving American freedom, our reserves of power are being depleted.

One sees this, for example, in the way that heightened claims of individual autonomy have eviscerated the concept of citizenship. Yesterday's civic obligations have become today's civic options. What once rated as duties—rallying to the country's defense at times of great emergency, for example—are now matters of choice. As individuals, Americans never cease to expect more. As members of a community, especially as members of a national community, they choose to contribute less.

Meanwhile, American political leaders—especially at the national level—have proven unable (or unwilling) to address the disparity between how much we want and what we can afford to pay. Successive administrations, abetted by Congress, have deepened a looming crisis of debt and dependency through unbridled spending. As Vice President Dick Cheney, a self-described conservative, announced when told that cutting taxes might be at odds with invading Iraq, "Deficits don't matter."[10] Politicians of both parties certainly act as if they don't.

Expectations that the world beyond our borders should accommodate the American way of life are hardly new. Since 9/11, however, our demands have become more insistent. In that regard, the neoconservative writer Robert Kagan is surely correct in observing that "America did not change on September 11. It only became more itself."[11] In the aftermath of the attacks on the World Trade Center and the Pentagon, Washington's resolve that nothing interfere with the individual American's pursuit of life, liberty, and happiness only hardened. That resolve found expression in the Bush administration's with-us-or-against-us rhetoric, in its disdain for the United Nations and traditional American allies, in its contempt for international law, and above all in its embrace of preventive war.

When President Bush declared in his second inaugural that the "survival of liberty in our land increasingly depends on the success of liberty in other lands," he was in effect claiming for the United States as freedom's chief agent the prerogative of waging war when and where it sees fit, those wars by definition being fought on freedom's behalf. In this sense, the Long War genuinely qualifies as a war to preserve the American way of life (centered on a specific conception of liberty) and simultaneously as a war to extend the American imperium (centered on dreams of a world remade in America's image), the former widely assumed to require the latter.

Yet, as events have made plain, the United States is ill-prepared to wage a global war of no exits and no deadlines. The sole superpower lacks the resources—economic, political, and military—to support a large-scale, protracted conflict without, at the very least, inflicting severe economic and political damage on itself. American power has limits and is inadequate to the ambitions to which hubris and sanctimony have given rise.

Here is the central paradox of our time: While the defense of American freedom seems to demand that U.S. troops fight in places like Iraq and Afghanistan, the exercise of that freedom at home undermines the nation's capacity to fight. A grand bazaar provides an inadequate basis upon which to erect a vast empire.

Meanwhile, a stubborn insistence on staying the course militarily ends up jeopardizing freedom at home. With Americans, even in wartime, refusing to curb their appetites, the Long War aggravates the economic contradictions that continue to produce debt and dependency. Moreover, a state of perpetual national security emergency aggravates the disorders afflicting our political system, allowing the executive branch to accrue ever more authority at the expense of the Congress and disfiguring the Constitution. In this sense, the Long War is both self-defeating and irrational.

Niebuhr once wrote, "One of the most pathetic aspects of human history is that every civilization expresses itself most pretentiously, compounds its partial and universal values most convincingly, and claims immortality for its finite existence at the very moment when the decay which leads to death has already begun."[12] Future generations of historians may well cite Niebuhr's dictum as a concise explanation of the folly that propelled the United States into its Long War.

In an immediate sense, it is the soldier who bears the burden of such folly. U.S. troops in battle dress and body armor, whom Americans profess to admire and support, pay the price for the nation's collective refusal to confront our domestic dysfunction. In many ways, the condition of the military today offers the most urgent expression of that dysfunction. Seven years into its confrontation with radical Islam, the United States finds itself with too much war for too few warriors—and with no prospect of producing the additional soldiers needed to close the gap. In effect, Americans now confront a looming military crisis to go along with the economic and political crises that they have labored so earnestly to ignore.

The Iraq War deserves our attention as the clearest manifestation of these three crises, demonstrating the extent to which they are inextricably linked and mutually reinforcing. That war was always unnecessary. Except in the eyes of the deluded and the disingenuous, it has long since become a fool's errand. Of perhaps even greater significance, it is both counterproductive and unsustainable.

Yet ironically Iraq may yet prove to be the source of our salvation. For the United States, the ongoing war makes plain the imperative of putting America's house in order. Iraq has revealed the futility of counting on military power to sustain our habits of profligacy. The day of reckoning approaches. Expending the lives of more American soldiers in hopes of deferring that day is profoundly wrong. History will not judge kindly a people who find nothing amiss in the prospect of endless armed conflict so long as they themselves are spared the effects. Nor will it view with favor an electorate that delivers political power into the hands of leaders unable to envision any alternative to perpetual war.

Rather than insisting that the world accommodate the United States, Americans need to reassert control over their own destiny, ending their condition of dependency and abandoning their imperial delusions. Of perhaps even greater difficulty, the combination of economic, political, and military crisis summons Americans to reexamine exactly what freedom entails. Soldiers cannot accomplish these tasks, nor should we expect politicians to do so. The onus of responsibility falls squarely on citizens.

1. The Crisis of Profligacy

Today, no less than in 1776, a passion for life, liberty, and the pursuit of happiness remains at the center of America's civic theology. The Jeffersonian trinity summarizes our common inheritance, defines our aspirations, and provides the touchstone for our influence abroad.

Yet if Americans still cherish the sentiments contained in Jefferson's Declaration of Independence, they have, over time, radically revised their understanding of those "inalienable rights." Today, individual Americans use their freedom to do many worthy things. Some read, write, paint, sculpt, compose, and play music. Others build, restore, and preserve. Still others attend plays, concerts, and sporting events, visit their local multiplexes, IM each other incessantly, and join "communities" of the like-minded in an ever-growing array of virtual worlds. They also pursue innumerable hobbies, worship, tithe, and, in commendably large numbers, attend to the needs of the less fortunate. Yet none of these in themselves define what it means to be an American in the twenty-first century.

If one were to choose a single word to characterize that identity, it would have to be *more*. For the majority of contemporary Americans, the essence of life, liberty, and the pursuit of happiness centers on a relentless personal quest to acquire, to consume, to indulge, and to shed whatever constraints might interfere with those endeavors. A bumper sticker, a sardonic motto, and a charge dating from the Age of Woodstock have recast the Jeffersonian trinity in modern vernacular: "Whoever dies with the most toys wins"; "Shop till you drop"; "If it feels good, do it."

It would be misleading to suggest that every American has surrendered to this ethic of self-gratification. Resistance to its demands persists and takes many forms. Yet dissenters, intent on curbing the American penchant for consumption and self-indulgence, are fighting a rear-guard action, valiant perhaps but unlikely to reverse the tide. The ethic of self-gratification has firmly entrenched itself as the defining feature of the American way of life. The point is neither to deplore nor to celebrate this fact, but simply to acknowledge it.

Others have described, dissected, and typically bemoaned the cultural—and even moral—implications of this development.[1] Few, however, have considered how an American preoccupation with "more" has affected U.S. relations with rest of the world. Yet the foreign policy implications of our present-day penchant for consumption and self-indulgence are almost entirely negative. Over the past six decades, efforts to satisfy spiraling consumer demand have given birth to a condition of profound dependency. The United States may still remain the mightiest power the world has ever seen, but the fact is that Americans are no longer masters of their own fate.

The ethic of self-gratification threatens the well-being of the United States. It does so not because Americans have lost touch with some mythical Puritan habits of hard work and self-abnegation, but because it saddles us with costly commitments abroad that we are increasingly ill-equipped to sustain while confronting us with dangers to which we have no ready response. As the prerequisites of the American way of life have grown, they have outstripped the means available to satisfy them. Americans of an earlier generation worried about bomber and missile gaps, both of which turned out to be fictitious. The present-day gap between requirements and the means available to satisfy those requirements is neither contrived nor imaginary. It is real and growing. This gap defines the crisis of American profligacy.

Power and Abundance

Placed in historical perspective, the triumph of this ethic of self-gratification hardly qualifies as a surprise. The restless search for a buck and the ruthless elimination of anyone—or anything—standing in the way of doing so have long been central to the American character. Touring the United States in the 1830s, Alexis de Tocqueville, astute observer of the young Republic, noted the "feverish ardor" of its citizens to accumulate. Yet, even as the typical American "clutches at everything," the Frenchman wrote, "he holds nothing fast, but soon loosens his grasp to pursue fresh gratifications." However munificent his possessions, the American hungered for more, an obsession that filled him with "anxiety, fear, and regret, and keeps his mind in ceaseless trepidation."[2]

Even in de Tocqueville's day, satisfying such yearnings as well as easing the anxieties and fears they evoked had important policy implications. To quench their ardor, Americans looked abroad, seeking to extend the reach of U.S. power. The pursuit of "fresh gratifications" expressed itself collectively in an urge to expand, territorially and commercially. This expansionist project was already well begun when de Tocqueville's famed *Democracy in America* appeared, most notably through Jefferson's acquisition of the Louisiana territory in 1803 and through ongoing efforts to remove (or simply eliminate) Native Americans, an undertaking that continued throughout the nineteenth century.

Preferring to remember their collective story somewhat differently, Americans look to politicians to sanitize their past. When, in his 2005 inaugural address, George W. Bush identified the promulgation of freedom as "the mission that created our nation," neoconservative hearts certainly beat a little faster, as they undoubtedly did when he went on to declare that America's "great liberating tradition" now required the United States to devote itself to "ending tyranny in our world." Yet Bush was simply putting his own gloss on a time-honored conviction ascribing to the United States a uniqueness of character and purpose. From its founding, America has expressed through its behavior and its evolution a providential purpose. Paying homage to, and therefore renewing, this tradition of American exceptionalism has long been one of the presidency's primary extraconstitutional obligations.

Many Americans find such sentiments compelling. Yet to credit the United States with possessing a "liberating tradition" is equivalent to saying that Hollywood has a "tradition of artistic excellence." The movie business is just that—a business. Its purpose is to make money. If once in a while a studio produces a film of aesthetic value, that may be cause for celebration, but profit, not revealing truth and beauty, defines the purpose of the enterprise.

Something of the same can be said of the enterprise launched on July 4, 1776. The hardheaded lawyers, merchants, farmers, and slaveholding plantation owners gathered in Philadelphia that summer did not set out to create a church. They founded a republic. Their purpose was not to save mankind. It was to ensure that people like themselves enjoyed unencumbered access to the Jeffersonian trinity.

In the years that followed, the United States achieved remarkable success in making good on those aims. Yet never during the course of America's transformation from a small power to a great one did the United States exert itself to liberate others—absent an overriding perception that the nation had large security or economic interests at stake.

From time to time, although not nearly as frequently as we like to imagine, some of the world's unfortunates managed as a consequence to escape from bondage. The Civil War did, for instance, produce emancipation. Yet to explain the conflagration of 1861–65 as a response to the plight of enslaved African Americans is to engage at best in an immense oversimplification. Near the end of World War II, GIs did liberate the surviving inmates of Nazi death camps. Yet for those who directed the American war effort of 1941–45, the fate of European Jews never figured as more than an afterthought.

Crediting the United States with a "great liberating tradition" distorts the past and obscures the actual motive force behind American politics and U.S. foreign policy. It transforms history into a morality tale, thereby providing a rationale for dodging serious moral analysis. To insist that the liberation of others has never been more than an ancillary motive of U.S. policy is not cynicism; it is a prerequisite to self-understanding.

If the young United States had a mission, it was not to liberate but to expand. "Of course," declared Theodore Roosevelt in 1899, as if explaining the self-evident to the obtuse, "our whole national history has been one of expansion." TR spoke truthfully. The founders viewed stasis as tantamount to suicide. From the outset, Americans evinced a compulsion to acquire territory and extend their commercial reach abroad.

How was expansion achieved? On this point, the historical record leaves no room for debate: by any means necessary. Depending on the circumstances, the United States relied on diplomacy, hard bargaining, bluster, chicanery, intimidation, or naked coercion. We infiltrated land belonging to our neighbors and then brazenly proclaimed it our own. We harassed, filibustered, and, when the situation called for it, launched full-scale invasions. We engaged in ethnic cleansing. At times, we insisted that treaties be considered sacrosanct. On other occasions, we blithely jettisoned solemn agreements that had outlived their usefulness.

As the methods employed varied, so too did the rationales offered to justify action. We touted our status as God's new Chosen People, erecting a "city upon a hill" destined to illuminate the world. We acted at the behest of providential guidance or responded to the urgings of our "manifest destiny." We declared our obligation to spread the gospel of Jesus Christ or to "uplift little brown brother." With Woodrow Wilson as our tutor, we shouldered our responsibility to "show the way to the nations of the world how they shall walk in the paths of liberty."[3] Critics who derided these claims as bunkum—the young Lincoln during the war with Mexico, Mark Twain after the imperial adventures of 1898,

Senator Robert La Follette amid "the war to end all wars"—
scored points but lost the argument. Periodically revised and
refurbished, American exceptionalism (which implied excep-
tional American prerogatives) only gained greater currency.

When it came to action rather than talk, even the policy
makers viewed as most idealistic remained fixated on one
overriding aim: enhancing American influence, wealth, and
power. The record of U.S. foreign relations from the earliest
colonial encounters with Native Americans to the end of the
Cold War is neither uniquely high-minded nor uniquely
hypocritical and exploitive. In this sense, the interpretations
of America's past offered by both George W. Bush and
Osama bin Laden fall equally wide of the mark. As a rising
power, the United States adhered to the iron laws of international politics, which allow little space for altruism. If the
tale of American expansion contains a moral theme at all,
that theme is necessarily one of ambiguity.

To be sure, the ascent of the United States did not occur
without missteps: opéra bouffe incursions into Canada;
William McKinley's ill-advised annexation of the Philippines; complicity in China's "century of humiliation"; disastrous post–World War I economic policies that paved the
way for the Great Depression; Harry Truman's decision in
1950 to send U.S. forces north of Korea's Thirty-eighth Parallel; among others. Most of these blunders and bonehead
moves Americans have long since shrugged off. Some, like
Vietnam, we find impossible to forget even as we persistently
disregard their implications.

However embarrassing, these missteps pale in significance when compared to the masterstrokes of American
presidential statecraft. In purchasing Louisiana from the
French, Thomas Jefferson may have overstepped the bounds
of his authority and in seizing California from Mexico, James

Polk may have perpetrated a war of conquest, but their actions ensured that the United States would one day become
a great power. To secure the isthmus of Panama, Theodore
Roosevelt orchestrated an outrageous swindle. The canal he
built there affirmed America's hemispheric dominion. In
collaborating with Joseph Stalin, FDR made common cause
with an indisputably evil figure. Yet this pact with the devil
destroyed the murderous Hitler while vaulting the United
States to a position of unquestioned global economic supremacy. A similar collaboration—forged by Richard Nixon
with the murderous Mao Zedong—helped bring down the
Soviet empire, thereby elevating the United States to the
self-proclaimed status of "sole superpower."

The achievements of these preeminent American statesmen derived not from their common devotion to a liberating
tradition but from boldness unburdened by excessive scru-
ples. Notwithstanding the high-sounding pronouncements
that routinely emanate from the White House and the State
Department, the defining characteristic of U.S. foreign policy
at its most successful has not been idealism, but pragmatism,
frequently laced with pragmatism's first cousin, opportunism.

What self-congratulatory textbooks once referred to as
America's "rise to power" did not unfold according to some
preconceived strategy for global preeminence. There was
never a secret blueprint or master plan. A keen eye for the
main chance, rather than fixed principles, guided policy. If
the means employed were not always pretty, the results
achieved were often stunning and paid enormous dividends
for the American people.

Expansion made the United States the "land of opportunity." From expansion came abundance. Out of abundance
came substantive freedom. Documents drafted in Philadelphia promised liberty. Making good on those promises re-

quired a political economy that facilitated the creation of wealth on an enormous scale.

Writing over a century ago, the historian Frederick Jackson Turner made the essential point. "Not the Constitution, but free land and an abundance of natural resources open to a fit people," he wrote, made American democracy possible.[4] A half century later, the historian David Potter discovered a similar symbiosis between affluence and liberty. "A politics of abundance," he claimed, had created the American way of life, "a politics which smiled both on those who valued abundance as a means to safeguard freedom and those who valued freedom as an aid in securing abundance."[5] William Appleman Williams, another historian, found an even tighter correlation. For Americans, he observed, "abundance was freedom and freedom was abundance."[6]

In short, expansion fostered prosperity, which in turn created the environment within which Americans pursued their dreams of freedom even as they argued with one another about just who deserved to share in that dream. The promise—and reality—of ever-increasing material abundance kept that argument within bounds. As the Industrial Revolution took hold, Americans came to count on an ever-larger economic pie to anesthetize the unruly and ameliorate tensions related to class, race, religion, and ethnicity. Money became the preferred lubricant for keeping social and political friction within tolerable limits. Americans, Reinhold Niebuhr once observed, "seek a solution for practically every problem of life in quantitative terms," certain that more is better.[7]

This reciprocal relationship between expansion, abundance, and freedom reached its apotheosis in the immediate aftermath of World War II. Assisted mightily by the fratricidal behavior of the traditional European powers through

two world wars and helped by reckless Japanese policies
that culminated in the attack on Pearl Harbor, the United
States emerged as a global superpower, while the American
people came to enjoy a standard of living that made them
the envy of the world. By 1945, the "American Century"
forecast by *Time-Life* publisher Henry Luce only four years
earlier seemed miraculously at hand. The United States was
the strongest, the richest, and—in the eyes of its white majority at least—the freest nation in all the world.

No people in history had ever ascended to such heights.
In order to gauge the ensuing descent—when the correlation
between expansion, abundance, and freedom diminished—
it is useful to recall the advantages the United States had
secured.

By the end of World War II, the country possessed nearly
two-thirds of the world's gold reserves and more than half
its entire manufacturing capacity.[8] In 1947, the United States
by itself accounted for one-third of world exports.[9] Its foreign
trade balance was comfortably in the black. As measured by
value, its exports more than doubled its imports.[10] The dollar had displaced the British pound sterling as *the* global
reserve currency, with the Bretton Woods system, the international monetary regime created in 1944, making the United
States the world's money manager. The country was, of
course, a net creditor. Among the world's producers of oil,
steel, airplanes, automobiles, and electronics, it ranked first
in each category. "Economically," wrote the historian Paul
Kennedy, "the world was its oyster."[11]

And that was only the beginning. Militarily, the United
States possessed unquestioned naval and air supremacy, un-
derscored until August 1949 by an absolute nuclear monopoly, affirmed thereafter by a permanent and indisputable
edge in military technology. The nation's immediate neigh-

bors were weak and posed no threat. Its adversaries were far away and possessed limited reach.

For the average American household, World War II had finally ended the Depression years. Fears that wartime-stoked prosperity might evaporate with the war itself proved groundless. Instead, the transition to peace touched off an unprecedented economic boom. In 1948, American per capita income exceeded by a factor of four the combined per capita income of Great Britain, France, West Germany, and Italy.[12] Wartime economic expansion—the gross national product grew by 60 percent between 1939 and 1945—had actually reduced economic inequality.[13] Greater income and pent-up demand now combined to create a huge domestic market that kept American factories humming and produced good jobs. As a consequence, the immediate postwar era became the golden age of the American middle class.

Postwar America was no utopia—far from it. Even in a time of bounty, a sizable portion of the population, above all African Americans, did not know either freedom or abundance. Yet lagging only a step or two behind the chronicle of American expansion abroad is a second narrative of expansion, which played itself out at home. The story it tells is one of Americans asserting their claims to full citizenship and making good on those claims so that over time freedom became not the privilege of the few but the birthright of the many. It too is a dramatic tale of achievement overlaid with ambiguity.

Who merits the privileges of citizenship? The answer prevailing in 1776—white male freeholders—was never satisfactory. By the stroke of a Jeffersonian pen, the Declaration of Independence had rendered such a narrow definition untenable. Pressures to amend that restricted concept of citizenship emerged almost immediately.

Until World War II, progress achieved on this front, though real, was fitful. During the years of the postwar economic boom, and especially during the 1960s, the floodgates opened. Barriers fell. The circle of freedom widened appreciably. The percentage of Americans marginalized as "second-class citizens" dwindled.

Many Americans remember the 1960s as the Freedom Decade—and with good cause. Although the modern civil rights movement predates that decade, it was then that the campaign for racial equality achieved its great breakthroughs, beginning in 1963 with the March on Washington and Martin Luther King's "I Have a Dream" speech. Women and gays followed suit. The founding of the National Organization for Women in 1966 signaled the reinvigoration of the fight for women's rights. In 1969, the Stonewall Uprising in New York City launched the gay rights movement.

Political credit for this achievement lies squarely with the Left. Abundance, sustained in no small measure by a postwar presumption of American "global leadership," made possible the expansion of freedom at home. Rebutting Soviet charges of racism and hypocrisy lent the promotion of freedom domestically a strategic dimension. Yet possibility only became reality thanks to progressive political activism.

Pick the group: blacks, Jews, women, Asians, Hispanics, working stiffs, gays, the handicapped—in every case, the impetus for providing equal access to the rights guaranteed by the Constitution originated among pinks, lefties, liberals, and bleeding-heart fellow travelers. When it came to ensuring that every American should get a fair shake, the contribution of modern conservatism has been essentially nil. Had Martin Luther King counted on William F. Buckley and the *National Review* to take up the fight against racial segregation in the 1950s and 1960s, Jim Crow would still be alive and well.

Granting the traditionally marginalized access to freedom constitutes a central theme of American politics since World War II. It does not diminish the credit due to those who engineered this achievement to note that their success stemmed, in part, from the fact that the United States was simultaneously asserting its claim to unquestioned global preeminence.

From World War II into the 1960s, more power abroad meant greater abundance at home, which, in turn, paved the way for greater freedom. The reformers who pushed and prodded for racial equality and women's rights did so in tacit alliance with the officials presiding over the postwar rehabilitation of Germany and Japan, with oil executives pressing to bring the Persian Gulf into America's sphere of influence, and with defense contractors urging the procurement of expensive new weaponry.

The creation, by the 1950s, of an informal American empire of global proportions was not the result of a conspiracy designed to benefit the few. Postwar foreign policy derived its legitimacy from a widely shared perception that power was being exercised abroad to facilitate the creation of a more perfect union at home. In this sense, General Curtis LeMay's nuclear strike force, the Strategic Air Command (SAC)—as a manifestation of American might as well as a central component of the postwar military-industrial complex—helped foster the conditions from which Betty Friedan's National Organization for Women emerged.

A proper understanding of contemporary history means acknowledging an ironic kinship between hard-bitten Cold Warriors like General LeMay and left-leaning feminists like Ms. Friedan. SAC helped make possible the feminine mystique and much else besides.

Not Less, But More

The two decades immediately following World War II marked the zenith of what the historian Charles Maier called "the Empire of Production."[14] During these years, unquestioned economic superiority endowed the United States with a high level of strategic self-sufficiency, translating in turn into remarkable freedom of action. In his Farewell Address, George Washington had dreamed of the day when the United States might acquire the strength sufficient "to give it, humanly speaking, the command of its own fortunes." Strength, the first president believed, would allow the nation to assert real independence, enabling Americans to "choose peace or war, as [their] interest, guided by justice, shall counsel." In the wake of World War II, that moment had emphatically arrived.

It soon passed. Even before 1950, the United States had begun to import foreign oil. At first, the quantities were trifling. Over time, they grew. Here was the canary in the economic mineshaft. Yet for two decades no one paid it much attention.

The empire of production continued churning out a never-ending array of goods, its preeminence seemingly permanent and beyond challenge. In Europe and East Asia, the United States showed commendable shrewdness in converting economic superiority into strategic advantage. In the twenty years following VJ Day, wrote Maier, "Americans traded wealth for preponderance," providing assistance to rebuild shattered economies in Western Europe and East Asia and opening up the U.S. market to their products.[15] America's postwar status as leader of the free world was bought and paid for in Washington.

In the 1960s, however, the empire of production began to

come undone. Within another twenty years—thanks to permanently negative trade balances, a crushing defeat in Vietnam, oil shocks, "stagflation," and the shredding of a moral consensus that could not withstand the successive assaults of Elvis Presley, "the pill," and the counterculture, along with news reports that God had died—it had become defunct. In its place, according to Maier, there emerged a new "Empire of Consumption." Just as the lunch-bucket-toting factory worker had symbolized the empire of production during its heyday, the teenager, daddy's credit card in her blue jeans and headed to the mall, now emerged as the empire of consumption's emblematic figure. The evil genius of the empire of production was Henry Ford. In the empire of consumption, Ford's counterpart was Walt Disney.

We can fix the tipping point with precision. It occurred between 1965, when President Lyndon Baines Johnson ordered U.S. combat troops to South Vietnam, and 1973, when President Richard M. Nixon finally ended direct U.S. involvement in that war. Prior to the Vietnam War, efforts to expand American power in order to promote American abundance usually proved conducive to American freedom. After Vietnam, efforts to expand American power continued; but when it came to either abundance or freedom, the results became increasingly problematic.

In retrospect, the economic indicators signaling an erosion of dominance seem obvious. The costs of the Vietnam War—and President Johnson's attempt to conceal them while pursuing his vision of a Great Society—destabilized the economy, as evidenced by deficits, inflation, and a weakening dollar. In August 1971, Nixon tacitly acknowledged the disarray into which the economy had fallen by devaluing the dollar and suspending its convertibility into gold.

That, of course, was only the beginning. Prior to the

1970s, because the United States had long been the world's number one producer of petroleum, American oil companies determined the global price of oil. In 1972, domestic oil production peaked and then began its inexorable, irreversible decline.[16] The year before, the prerogative of setting the price of crude oil had passed into the hands of a new producers' group, the Organization of the Petroleum Exporting Countries (OPEC).[17]

With U.S. demand for oil steadily increasing, so, too, did overall American reliance on imports. Simultaneously, a shift in the overall terms of trade occurred. In 1971, after decades in the black, the United States had a negative trade balance. In 1973, and again in 1975, exports exceeded imports in value. From then on, it was all red ink; never again would American exports equal imports. In fact, the gap between the two grew at an ever-accelerating rate year by year.[18] For the American public, the clearest and most painful affirmation of the nation's sudden economic vulnerability came with the "oil shock" of 1973, which produced a 40 percent spike in gas prices, long lines at filling stations, and painful shortages.

By the late 1970s, a period of slow growth and high inflation, the still-forming crisis of profligacy was already causing real distress in American households. The first protracted economic downturn since World War II confronted Americans with a fundamental choice. They could curb their appetites and learn to live within their means or deploy dwindling reserves of U.S. power in hopes of obliging others to accommodate their penchant for conspicuous consumption. Between July 1979 and March 1983, a fateful interval bookended by two memorable presidential speeches, they opted decisively for the latter.

Here lies the true pivot of contemporary American history, far more relevant to our present predicament than sup-posedly decisive events like the fall of the Berlin Wall or the collapse of the Soviet Union. Between the summer of 1979 and the spring of 1983, "global leadership," the signature claim of U.S. foreign policy, underwent a subtle transforma-tion. Although the United States kept up the pretense that the rest of the world could not manage without its guidance and protection, leadership became less a choice than an im-perative. The exercise of global primacy offered a way of compensating for the erosion of a previously dominant eco-nomic position. Yet whatever deference Washington was able to command could not conceal the extent to which the United States itself was becoming increasingly beholden to others. Leadership now carried connotations of dependence.

On July 15, 1979, Jimmy Carter delivered the first of those two pivotal speeches. Although widely regarded in our own day as a failed, even a hapless, president, Carter, in this instance at least, demonstrated remarkable foresight. He not only appreciated the looming implications of de-pendence but also anticipated the consequences of allowing this condition to fester.

The circumstances for Carter's speech were less than congenial. In the summer of 1979, popular dissatisfaction with his presidency was growing at an alarming rate. The economy was in terrible shape. Inflation had reached 11 per-cent. Seven percent of American workers were unemployed. The prime lending rate stood at 15 percent and was still ris-ing. By postwar standards, all of these figures were unac-ceptably high, if not unprecedented. Worse yet, in January 1979, Iranian revolutionaries ousted the shah of Iran, a long-time U.S. ally, resulting in a second "oil shock." Gasoline prices in the United States soared, due not to actual short-ages but to panic buying. The presidential election season beckoned. If Carter hoped to win a second term, he needed to turn things around quickly.

The president had originally intended to speak on July 5, focusing his address exclusively on energy. At the last minute, he decided to postpone it. Instead, he spent ten days sequestered at Camp David, using the time, he explained, "to reach out and listen to the voices of America." At his invitation, a host of politicians, academics, business and labor leaders, clergy, and private citizens trooped through the presidential retreat to offer their views on what was wrong with America and what Carter needed to do to set things right. The result combined a seminar of sorts with an exercise in self-flagellation.

The speech that Carter delivered when he returned to the White House bore little resemblance to the one he had planned to give ten days earlier. He began by explaining that he had decided to look beyond energy because "the true problems of our Nation are much deeper." The energy crisis of 1979, he suggested, was merely a symptom of a far greater crisis. "So, I want to speak to you first tonight about a subject even more serious than energy or inflation. I want to talk to you right now about a fundamental threat to American democracy."

In short order, Carter then proceeded to kill any chance he had of securing reelection. In American political discourse, fundamental threats are by definition external. Nazi Germany, Imperial Japan, or international communism could threaten the United States. That very year, Iran's Islamic revolutionaries had emerged to pose another such threat. That the actions of everyday Americans might pose a comparable threat amounted to rank heresy. Yet Carter now dared to suggest that the real danger to American democracy lay within.

The nation as a whole was experiencing "a crisis of confidence," he announced. "It is a crisis that strikes at the very heart and soul and spirit of our national will. We can see this crisis in the growing doubt about the meaning of our own lives and in the loss of a unity of purpose for our nation." This erosion of confidence threatened "to destroy the social and the political fabric of America."

Americans had strayed from the path of righteousness. "In a nation that was proud of hard work, strong families, close-knit communities, and our faith in God," the president continued,

> too many of us now tend to worship self-indulgence and consumption. Human identity is no longer defined by what one does, but by what one owns. But we've discovered that owning things and consuming things does not satisfy our longing for meaning. We've learned that piling up material goods cannot fill the emptiness of lives which have no confidence or purpose.

In other words, the spreading American crisis of confidence was an outward manifestation of an underlying crisis of values. With his references to what "we've discovered" and what "we've learned," Carter implied that he was merely voicing concerns that his listeners already shared: that average Americans viewed their lives as empty, unsatisfying rituals of buying, and longed for something more meaningful.

To expect Washington to address these concerns was, he made clear, fanciful. According to the president, the federal government had become "an island," isolated from the people. Its major institutions were paralyzed and corrupt. It was "a system of government that seems incapable of action."

Carter spoke of "a Congress twisted and pulled in every direction by hundreds of well financed and powerful special interests." Partisanship routinely trumped any concern for the common good: "You see every extreme position defended to the last vote, almost to the last breath by one unyielding group or another."

"We are at a turning point in our history," Carter announced.

> There are two paths to choose. One is a path I've warned about tonight, the path that leads to fragmentation and self-interest. Down that road lies a mistaken idea of freedom, the right to grasp for ourselves some advantage over others. That path would be one of constant conflict between narrow interests ending in chaos and immobility.

The continued pursuit of this mistaken idea of freedom was "a certain route to failure." The alternative—a course consistent with "all the traditions of our past [and] all the lessons of our heritage"—pointed down "another path, the path of common purpose and the restoration of American values." Down that path, the president claimed, lay "true freedom for our Nation and ourselves."

As portrayed by Carter, the mistaken idea of freedom was quantitative: It centered on the never-ending quest for more while exalting narrow self-interest. His conception of authentic freedom was qualitative: It meant living in accordance with permanent values. At least by implication, it meant settling for less.

How Americans dealt with the question of energy, the president believed, was likely to determine which idea of freedom would prevail. "Energy will be the immediate test of our ability to unite this Nation, and it can also be the standard around which we rally." By raising that standard, Carter insisted, "we can seize control again of our common destiny." With this in mind, Carter outlined a six-point program designed to end what he called "this intolerable dependence on foreign oil." He promised action to reduce oil imports by one-half within a decade. In the near term, he vowed to establish quotas capping the amount of oil coming into the country. He called for a national effort to develop alternative energy sources. He proposed legislation mandating reductions in the amount of oil used for power generation. He advocated establishment of a new federal agency "to cut through the red tape, the delays, and the endless roadblocks to completing key energy projects." And finally, he summoned the American people to conserve: "to take no unnecessary trips, to use carpools or public transportation whenever you can, to park your car one extra day per week, to obey the speed limit, and to set your thermostats to save fuel."

Although Carter expressed confidence that the United States could one day regain its energy independence, he acknowledged that in the near term "there [was] simply no way to avoid sacrifice." Indeed, implicit in Carter's speech was the suggestion that sacrifice just might be a good thing. For the sinner, some sort of penance must necessarily precede redemption.

The response to his address—instantly labeled the "malaise" speech although Carter never used that word—was tepid at best. Carter's remarks had blended religiosity and populism in ways that some found off-putting. Writing in the *New York Times,* Francis X. Clines called it the "cross-of-malaise" speech, comparing it unfavorably to the famous "cross-of-gold" oration that had vaulted William Jennings Bryan to political prominence many decades earlier.[19] Others

criticized what they saw as a penchant for anguished moral-
izing and a tendency to find fault everywhere except in his
own White House. In the *New York Times Magazine,* Professor Eugene Kennedy mocked "Carter Agonistes," depicting
the president as a "distressed angel, passing judgment on us
all, and speaking solemnly not of blood and sweat but of oil
and sin."[20]

As an effort to reorient public policy, Carter's appeal
failed completely. Americans showed little enthusiasm for
the president's brand of freedom with its connotations of
virtuous austerity. Presented with an alternative to quantitative solutions, to the search for "more," they declined the offer. Not liking the message, Americans shot the messenger.
Given the choice, more still looked better.

Carter's crisis-of-confidence speech did enjoy a long and
fruitful life—chiefly as fodder for his political opponents.
The most formidable of them, already the front-runner for
the 1980 Republican nomination, was Ronald Reagan, the
former governor of California. Reagan portrayed himself as
conservative. He was, in fact, the modern prophet of profligacy, the politician who gave moral sanction to the empire
of consumption. Beguiling his fellow citizens with his talk of
"morning in America," the faux-conservative Reagan added
to America's civic religion two crucial beliefs: Credit has no
limits, and the bills will never come due. Balance the books,
pay as you go, save for a rainy day—Reagan's abrogation of
these ancient bits of folk wisdom did as much to recast America's moral constitution as did sex, drugs, and rock and roll.

Reagan offered his preliminary response to Carter on
November 13, 1979, the day he officially declared himself a
candidate for the presidency. When it came to confidence,
the former governor wanted it known that he had lots of it.
In a jab at Carter, he alluded to those "who would have us

believe that the United States, like other great civilizations of the past, has reached the zenith of its power" and who "tell us we must learn to live with less." Reagan rejected these propositions. He envisioned a future in which the United States would gain even greater power while Americans would enjoy ever greater prosperity, the one reinforcing the other. The sole obstacle to all this was the federal government, which he characterized as inept, arrogant, and confiscatory. His proposed solution was to pare down the bureaucracy, reduce federal spending, and cut taxes.

If there was an energy crisis, that too—he made clear—was the government's fault. On one point at least, Reagan agreed with Carter: "The only way to free ourselves from the monopoly pricing power of OPEC is to be less dependent on outside sources of fuel." Yet Reagan had no interest in promoting energy independence through reduced consumption. "The answer, obvious to anyone except those in the administration it seems, is more domestic production of oil and gas." When it came to energy, he was insistent: "We must decide that 'less' is not enough."

History remembers Reagan as a fervent Cold Warrior. Yet, in announcing his candidacy, he devoted remarkably little attention to the Soviet Union. In referring to the Kremlin, his language was measured, not belligerent. He did not denounce the Soviets for being "evil." He made no allusions to rolling back communism. He offered no tribute to the American soldier standing guard on freedom's frontiers. He said nothing about an urgent need to rebuild America's defenses. In outlining his views on foreign policy, he focused primarily on his vision of a "North American accord," an economic union linking the United States, Canada, and Mexico. "It is time we stopped thinking of our nearest neighbors as foreigners," he declared.

As was so often the case, Reagan laid on enough frosting to compensate for any shortcomings in the cake. In his peroration, he approvingly quoted Tom Paine on Americans having the power to "begin the world over again." He endorsed John Winthrop's charge that God had commanded Americans to erect "a city upon a hill." And he cited (without attribution) Franklin D. Roosevelt's entreaty for the present generation of Americans to keep their "rendezvous with destiny." For Reagan, the arc of America's future, like the arc of the American past (at least as he remembered it), pointed ever upward. Overall, it was a bravura performance.

And it worked. No doubt Reagan spoke from the heart, but his real gift was a canny knack for telling Americans what most of them wanted to hear. As a candidate for the White House, Reagan did not call on Americans to tighten their belts, make do, or settle for less. He saw no need for sacrifice or self-denial. He rejected as false Carter's dichotomy between quantity and quality. Above all, he assured his countrymen that they could have more. Throughout his campaign, this remained a key theme.

The contest itself took place against the backdrop of the ongoing hostage crisis that saw several dozen American diplomats and soldiers held prisoner in Iran. Here was unmistakable evidence of what happened when the United States hesitated to assert itself in this part of the world. The lesson seemed clear: If developments in the Persian Gulf could adversely affect the American standard of living, then control of that region by anyone other than the United States had become intolerable. Carter himself was the first to make this point, when he enunciated the Carter Doctrine in January 1980, vowing to use "any means necessary, including military force," to prevent a hostile power from dominating the region.

Carter's eleventh-hour pugnacity came too late to save his presidency. The election of 1980 reaffirmed a continuing American preference for quantitative solutions. Despite the advantages of incumbency, Carter suffered a crushing defeat. Reagan carried all but four states and won the popular vote by well over eight million. It was a landslide and a portent.

On January 20, 1981, Ronald Reagan became president. His inaugural address served as an occasion to recite various conservative bromides. Reagan made a show of decrying the profligacy of the recent past. "For decades we have piled deficit upon deficit, mortgaging our future and our children's future for the temporary convenience of the present. To continue this long trend is to guarantee tremendous social, cultural, political, and economic upheavals." He vowed to put America's economic house in order. "You and I, as individuals, can, by borrowing, live beyond our means, but for only a limited period of time. Why, then, should we think that collectively, as a nation, we're not bound by that same limitation?" Reagan reiterated an oft-made promise "to check and reverse the growth of government."

He would do none of these things. In each case, in fact, he did just the reverse. During the Carter years, the federal deficit had averaged $54.5 billion annually. During the Reagan era, deficits skyrocketed, averaging $210.6 billion over the course of Reagan's two terms in office. Overall federal spending nearly doubled, from $590.9 billion in 1980 to $1.14 trillion in 1989.[21] The federal government did not shrink. It grew, the bureaucracy swelling by nearly 5 percent while Reagan occupied the White House.[22] Although his supporters had promised that he would shut down extraneous government programs and agencies, that turned out to be just so much hot air.

To call Reagan a phony or a hypocrite is to miss the

point. The Reagan Revolution over which he presided was never about fiscal responsibility or small government. The object of the exercise was to give the American people what they wanted, that being the essential precondition for winning reelection in 1984 and consolidating Republican control in Washington. Far more accurately than Jimmy Carter, Reagan understood what made Americans tick: They wanted self-gratification, not self-denial. Although always careful to embroider his speeches with inspirational homilies and testimonials to old-fashioned virtues, Reagan mainly indulged American self-indulgence.

Reagan's two terms in office became an era of gaudy prosperity and excess. Tax cuts and the largest increase to date in peacetime military spending formed the twin centerpieces of Reagan's economic policy, the former justified by theories of supply-side economics, the latter by the perceived imperative of responding to a Soviet arms buildup and Soviet adventurism. Declaring that "defense is not a budget item," Reagan severed the connection between military spending and all other fiscal or political considerations—a proposition revived by George W. Bush after September 2001.

None of this is to suggest that claims of a Reagan Revolution were fraudulent. There was a revolution; it just had little to do with the advertised tenets of conservatism. The true nature of the revolution becomes apparent only in retrospect. Reagan unveiled it in remarks that he made on March 23, 1983, a speech in which the president definitively spelled out his alternative to Carter's road not taken.

History remembers this as the occasion when the president announced his Strategic Defense Initiative—a futuristic "impermeable" antimissile shield intended to make nuclear weapons "impotent and obsolete." Critics derisively dubbed his proposal "Star Wars," a label the president, in the end, embraced. ("If you will pardon my stealing a film line—the Force is with us.") Yet embedded in Reagan's remarks were two decidedly radical propositions: first, that the minimum requirements of U.S. security now required the United States to achieve a status akin to invulnerability; and second, that modern technology was bringing this seemingly utopian goal within reach. Star Wars, in short, introduced into mainstream politics the proposition that Americans could be truly safe only if the United States enjoyed something akin to permanent global military supremacy. Here was Reagan's preferred response to the crisis that Jimmy Carter had identified in July 1979. Here, too, can be found the strategic underpinnings of George W. Bush's post-9/11 global war on terror. SDI prefigured the GWOT, both resting on the assumption that military power offered an antidote to the uncertainties and anxieties of living in a world not run entirely in accordance with American preferences.

Whereas President Carter had summoned Americans to mend their ways, which implied a need for critical self-awareness, President Reagan obviated any need for soul-searching by simply inviting his fellow citizens to carry on. For Carter, ending American dependence on foreign oil meant promoting moral renewal at home. Reagan—and Reagan's successors—mimicked Carter in bemoaning the nation's growing energy dependence. In practice, however, they did next to nothing to curtail that dependence. Instead, they wielded U.S. military power to ensure access to oil, hoping thereby to prolong the empire of consumption's lease on life. Carter had portrayed quantity (the American preoccupation with what he had called "piling up material goods") as fundamentally at odds with quality (authentic freedom as he defined it). Reagan reconciled what was, to Carter, increasingly irreconcilable. In Reagan's view, quality (advanced technology converted to military use by talented, highly skilled soldiers) could sustain quantity (a consumer economy based on the availability of cheap credit and cheap oil).

Pledges of benign intent concealed the full implications of Star Wars. To skeptics—nuclear strategists worried that the pursuit of strategic defenses might prove "destabilizing"— Reagan offered categorical assurances. "The defense policy of the United States is based on a simple premise: The United States does not start fights. We will never be an aggressor. We maintain our strength in order to deter and defend against aggression—to preserve freedom and peace." According to Reagan, the employment of U.S. forces for anything but defensive purposes was simply inconceivable. "Every item in our defense program—our ships, our tanks, our planes, our funds for training and spare parts—is intended for one all-important purpose: to keep the peace."

Reinhold Niebuhr once observed that "the most significant moral characteristic of a nation is its hypocrisy."[23] In international politics, the chief danger of hypocrisy is that it inhibits self-understanding. The hypocrite ends up fooling mainly himself.

Whether or not, in 1983, Ronald Reagan sincerely believed that "the United States does not start fights" and by its nature could not commit acts of aggression is impossible to say. He would hardly have been the first politician who came to believe what it was expedient for him to believe. What we can say with certainty is that events in our own time, most notably the Iraq War, have refuted Reagan's assurances, with fateful consequences.

Illusions about military power first fostered by Reagan outlived his presidency. Unambiguous global military supremacy became a standing aspiration; for the Pentagon, anything less than unquestioned dominance now qualified as dangerously inadequate. By the 1990s, the conviction that advanced technology held the key to unlocking hitherto undreamed-of military capabilities had moved from the heavens to the earth.

A new national security consensus emerged based on the conviction that the United States military could dominate the planet as Reagan had proposed to dominate outer space. In Washington, confidence that a high-quality military establishment, dexterously employed, could enable the United States, always with high-minded intentions, to organize the world to its liking had essentially become a self-evident truth. In this malignant expectation—not in any of the conservative ideals for which he is retrospectively venerated—lies the essence of the Reagan legacy.

Taking the Plunge

Just beneath the glitter of the Reagan years, the economic position of the United States continued to deteriorate. Despite the president's promise to restore energy independence, reliance on imported oil soared. By the end of Reagan's presidency, 41 percent of the oil consumed domestically came from abroad. It was during his first term that growing demand for Chinese goods produced the first negative trade balance with that country. In the same period, Washington—and the American people more generally—resorted to borrowing. Through the 1970s, economic growth had enabled the United States to reduce the size of a national debt (largely accrued during World War II) relative to the overall gross national product (GNP). At the beginning of the Reagan presidency, that ratio stood at a relatively modest 31.5 percent of GNP, the lowest since 1931. Reagan's huge deficits reversed that trend.

The United States had long touted its status as a creditor

nation as a symbol of overall economic strength. That, too, ended in the Reagan era. In 1986, the net international investment position of the United States turned negative as U.S. assets owned by foreigners exceeded the assets that Americans owned abroad. The imbalance has continued to grow ever since.[24] Even as the United States began accumulating trillions of dollars of debt, the inclination of individual Americans to save began to disappear. For most of the postwar era, personal savings had averaged a robust 8–10 percent of disposable income. In 1985, that figure began a gradual slide toward zero.[25] Simultaneously, consumer debt increased, so that by the end of the century household debt exceeded household income.[26]

American profligacy during the 1980s had a powerful effect on foreign policy. The impact manifested itself in two ways. On the one hand, Reagan's willingness to spend without limit helped bring the Cold War to a peaceful conclusion. On the other hand, American habits of conspicuous consumption, encouraged by Reagan, drew the United States ever more deeply into the vortex of the Islamic world, saddling an increasingly debt-ridden and energy-dependent nation with commitments that it could neither shed nor sustain. By expending huge sums on an arsenal of high-tech weapons, Reagan nudged the Kremlin toward the realization that the Soviet Union could no longer compete with the West. By doing nothing to check the country's reliance on foreign oil, he laid a trap into which his successors would stumble. If Reagan deserves plaudits for the former, he also deserves to be held accountable for the latter.

Yet it would be a mistake to imply that there were two Reagans—the one a farsighted statesman who won the Cold War, the other a chucklehead who bollixed up U.S. relations with the Islamic world. Cold War policy and Middle East-

ern policy did not exist in separate compartments; they
were intimately, if perversely, connected. To employ the
formulation preferred by Norman Podhoretz and other
neoconservatives—viewing the Cold War and the global
war on terror as successors to World Wars I and II—Reagan-
era exertions undertaken to win "World War III" inadvertently paved the way for "World War IV," while leaving the
United States in an appreciably weaker position to conduct
that struggle.

The relationship between World Wars III and IV becomes
apparent when recalling Reagan's policy toward Afghanistan and Iraq—the former a seemingly brilliant success that
within a decade gave birth to a quagmire, the latter a cynical gambit that backfired, touching off a sequence of events
that would culminate in a stupendous disaster.

As noted in the final report of the National Commission
on Terrorist Attacks Upon the United States, "A decade of
conflict in Afghanistan, from 1979 to 1989, gave Islamist extremists a rallying point and a training field."[27] The com-
missioners understate the case. In Afghanistan, jihadists
took on a superpower, the Soviet Union, and won. They
gained immeasurably in confidence and ambition, their efforts funded in large measure by the American taxpayer.

The billions that Reagan spent funneling weapons, am-
munition, and other support to the Afghan mujahideen were
as nothing compared to the $1.2 trillion his administration
expended modernizing U.S. military forces. Yet American
policy in Afghanistan during the 1980s illustrates the Reagan
Doctrine in its purest form. In the eyes of Reagan's admirers, it was his masterstroke, a bold and successful effort to
roll back the Soviet empire. The exploits of the Afghan "resistance" fired the president's imagination, and he offered the
jihadists unstinting and enthusiastic support. In designating

March 21, 1982, "Afghanistan Day," for example, Reagan proclaimed, "The freedom fighters of Afghanistan are defending principles of independence and freedom that form the basis of global security and stability."[28]

In point of fact, these "freedom fighters" had no interest at all in global security and stability. Reagan's depiction of their aims inverted the truth, as events soon demonstrated. Once the Soviets departed from Afghanistan, a vicious civil war ensued with radical Islamists—the Taliban—eventually emerging victorious. The Taliban, in turn, provided sanctuary to Al Qaeda. From Taliban-controlled Afghanistan, Osama bin Laden plotted his holy war against the United States. After the attacks of September 11, 2001, the United States rediscovered Afghanistan, overthrew the Taliban, and then stayed on, intent on creating a state aligned with the West. A mere dozen years after the Kremlin had thrown in the towel, U.S. troops found themselves in a position not unlike that of Soviet soldiers in the 1980s—outsiders attempting to impose a political order on a fractious population animated by an almost pathological antipathy toward foreign occupiers.

As long as it had remained, however tenuously, within the Kremlin's sphere of influence, Afghanistan posed no threat to the United States, just as, before 1980, the five Central Asian republics of the Soviet Union, forming a crescent north of Afghanistan, hardly registered on the Pentagon's meter of strategic priorities (or American consciousness). Once the Soviets were ousted from Afghanistan in 1989 and the Soviet Union itself collapsed two years later, all that began to change. In the wake of the 9/11 attacks, planned in Afghanistan, all of "Central Asia suddenly became valuable real estate to the United States."[29] In a sort of reverse domino theory, the importance now attributed to Afghanistan increased the importance of the entire region. After September 2001, U.S.

officials and analysts began using terms like *strategic, crucial,* and *critical* when referring to Central Asia. Here was yet another large swath of territory to which American interests obliged the United States to attend. So the ripples caused by Reagan's Afghanistan policy continued to spread.

Distracted by the "big war" in Iraq and the "lesser war" in Afghanistan, Americans have paid remarkably little attention to this story. Yet the evolution of military policy in relation to the "stans" of the former Soviet Union nicely illustrates the extent to which a foreign policy tradition of reflexive expansionism remains alive, long after it has ceased to make sense.

In the Clinton years, the Pentagon had already begun to express interest in Central Asia, conducting "peacekeeping exercises" in the former Soviet republics and establishing military-to-military exchange programs. In 2001, in conjunction with the U.S. invasion of Afghanistan, the Bush administration launched far more intensive efforts to carve out a foothold for American power across Central Asia.

Pentagon initiatives in the region still fall under the official rubric of *engagement.* This anodyne term encompasses a panoply of activities that, since 2001, have included recurring training missions, exercises, and war games; routine visits to the region by senior military officers and Defense Department civilians; and generous "security assistance" subsidies to train and equip local military forces. The purpose of engagement is to increase U.S. influence, especially over regional security establishments, facilitating access to the region by U.S. forces and thereby laying the groundwork for future interventions. With an eye toward the latter, the Pentagon has negotiated overflight rights as well as securing permission to use local facilities in several Central Asian republics. At Manas in Kyrgyzstan, the United States maintains a permanent air base, established in December 2001.

The U.S. military presence in Central Asia is a work in progress. Along with successes, there have been setbacks, to include being thrown out of Uzbekistan. Yet as analysts discuss next steps, the terms of the debate are telling. Disagreement may exist on the optimum size of the U.S. "footprint" in the region, but a consensus has formed in Washington around the proposition that some long-term presence *is* essential. Observers debate the relative merits of permanent bases versus "semiwarm" facilities, but they take it as a given that U.S. forces require the ability to operate throughout the area.

We've been down this path before. After liberating Cuba in 1898 and converting it into a protectorate, the United States set out to transform the entire Caribbean into an "American lake." Just as, a century ago, senior U.S. officials proclaimed their concern for the well-being of Haitians, Dominicans, and Nicaraguans, so do senior U.S. officials now insist on their commitment to "economic reform, democratic reform, and human rights" for all Central Asians.[30]

But this is mere camouflage. The truth is that the United States is engaged in an effort to incorporate Central Asia into the Pax Americana. Whereas expansion into the Caribbean a century ago paid economic dividends as well as enhancing U.S. security, expansion into Central Asia is unlikely to produce comparable benefits. It will cost far more than it will ever return.

American officials may no longer refer to Afghan warlords and insurgents as "freedom fighters"; yet, to a very large degree, U.S. and NATO forces in present-day Afghanistan are fighting the offspring of the jihadists that Reagan so lavishly supported in the 1980s. Preferring to compartmentalize history into pre-9/11 and post-9/11 segments, Americans remain oblivious to the consequences that grew out of Ronald Reagan's collaboration with the mujahideen.

Seldom has a seemingly successful partnership so quickly yielded poisonous fruit. In retrospect, the results achieved by liberating Afghanistan in 1989 serve as a cosmic affirmation of Reinhold Niebuhr's entire worldview. Of Afghanistan in the wake of the Soviet withdrawal, truly it can be said, as he wrote long ago, "The paths of progress . . . proved to be more devious and unpredictable than the putative managers of history could understand."[31]

When it came to the Persian Gulf, Reagan's profligacy took a different form. Far more than any of his predecessors, Reagan led the United States down the road to Persian Gulf perdition. History will hold George W. Bush primarily accountable for the disastrous Iraq War of 2003. But if that war had a godfather, it was Ronald Reagan.

Committed to quantitative solutions, Reagan never questioned the proposition that the American way of life required ever-larger quantities of energy, especially oil. Since satisfying American demand by expanding domestic oil production was never anything but a mirage, Reagan instead crafted policies intended to alleviate the risks associated with dependency. To prevent any recurrence of the oil shocks of 1973 and 1979, he put in motion efforts to secure U.S. dominion over the Persian Gulf. A much-hyped but actually receding Soviet threat provided the rationale for the Reagan military buildup of the 1980s. Ironically, however, the splendid army that Reagan helped create found eventual employment not in defending the West against totalitarianism but in vainly trying to impose an American imperium on the Persian Gulf.

To credit Reagan with having conceived a full-fledged Persian Gulf strategy would go too far. Indeed, his administration's immediate response to various crises roiling the region produced a stew of incoherence. In Lebanon, he flung

away the lives of 241 marines in a 1983 mission that still de-
fies explanation. The alacrity with which he withdrew U.S.
forces from Beirut after a suicide truck bomb had leveled a
marine barracks there suggests that there really was no mission at all.

Yet Reagan's failed intervention in Lebanon seems positively logical compared to the contradictions riddling his
policies toward Iran and Iraq. Saddam Hussein's invasion
of Iran touched off a brutal war that spanned Reagan's presidency. When the Islamic republic seemed likely to win that
conflict, Reagan famously "tilted" in favor of Iraq, providing intelligence, loan guarantees, and other support while
turning a blind eye to Saddam's crimes. American assistance to Iraq did not enable Saddam to defeat Iran; it just
kept the war going. At about the same time, in what became
known as the Iran-Contra Affair, White House operatives
secretly and illegally provided weapons to Saddam's enemies, the ayatollahs ruling Iran, who were otherwise said to
represent a dire threat to U.S. national security.

For all the attention they eventually attracted, these mis-
adventures served primarily to divert attention from the
central thrust of Reagan's Persian Gulf policy. The story
lurking behind the headlines was one of strategic reorientation: During the 1980s, the Pentagon began gearing up for
large-scale and sustained military operations in the region.

This reorientation actually began in the waning days of
the Carter administration, when President Carter publicly
declared control of the Persian Gulf to be a vital interest.
Not since the Tonkin Gulf Resolution has a major statement
of policy been the source of greater mischief. Yet for Reagan
and for each of his successors, the Carter Doctrine has remained a sacred text, never questioned, never subject to re-
assessment. As such, it has provided the overarching

rationale for nearly thirty years of ever-intensifying military activism in the Persian Gulf.

Even so, when Reagan succeeded Carter in January 1981, U.S. forces possessed only the most rudimentary ability to intervene in the Gulf. By the time he left office eight years later, he had positioned the United States to assert explicit military preponderance in the region—as reflected in war plans and exercises, the creation of new command structures, the development of critical infrastructure, the prepositioning of equipment stocks, and the acquisition of basing and overflight rights.[32] Prior to 1981, the Persian Gulf had lagged behind Western Europe and Northeast Asia in the Pentagon's hierarchy of strategic priorities. By 1989, it had pulled even. Soon thereafter, it became priority number one.

The strategic reorientation that Reagan orchestrated encouraged the belief that military power could extend indefinitely America's profligate expenditure of energy. Simply put, the United States would rely on military might to keep order in the Gulf and maintain the flow of oil, thereby mitigating the implications of American energy dependence. By the time that Reagan retired from office, this had become the basis for national security strategy in the region.

Reagan himself had given this new strategy a trial run of sorts. U.S. involvement in the so-called Tanker War, now all but forgotten, provided a harbinger of things to come. As an ancillary part of their war of attrition, Iran and Iraq had begun targeting each other's shipping in the Gulf. Attacks soon extended to neutral vessels, with each country determined to shut down its adversary's ability to export oil.

Intent on ensuring that the oil would keep flowing, Reagan reinforced the U.S. naval presence in the region. The waters of the Gulf became increasingly crowded. Then in May 1987, an Iraqi missile slammed into the frigate USS

Stark, killing thirty-seven sailors. Saddam Hussein described the attack as an accident and apologized. Reagan generously accepted Saddam's explanation and blamed Iran for the escalating violence.

That same year, Washington responded favorably to a Kuwaiti request for the U.S. Navy to protect its tanker fleet. When, in the course of escort operations in April 1988, the USS *Samuel B. Roberts* struck an Iranian mine, suffering serious damage, Reagan upped the ante. U.S. forces began conducting attacks on Iranian warships, naval facilities, and oil platforms used for staging military operations. Iranian naval operations in the Gulf soon ceased, although not before an American warship had mistakenly shot down an Iranian commercial airliner, with the loss of nearly three hundred civilians.

The Reagan administration congratulated itself on having achieved a handsome victory. For a relatively modest investment—the thirty-seven American sailors killed on the *Stark* were forgotten almost as quickly as the doomed passengers on Iran Air Flight 655—the United States had seemingly demonstrated its ability to keep open the world's oil lifeline. But appearance belied a more complex reality. From the outset, Saddam Hussein had been the chief perpetrator of the Tanker War. Reagan's principal accomplishment had been to lend Saddam a helping hand—at substantial moral cost to the United States.

The president's real achievement in the Persian Gulf was to make a down payment on an enterprise destined to consume tens of thousands of lives, many American, many others not, along with hundreds of billions of dollars—to date at least, the ultimate expression of American profligacy.

Whatever their professed ideological allegiance or party preference, Reagan's successors have all adhered to the now hallowed tradition of decrying America's energy dependence. In 2006, this ritual reached a culminating point of sorts when George W. Bush announced, "America is addicted to oil." Yet none of Reagan's successors have taken any meaningful action to address this addiction. Each tacitly endorsed it, essentially acknowledging that dependence had become an integral part of American life. Like Reagan, each of his successors ignored pressing questions about the costs that dependence entailed.

That Americans might shake the habit by choosing a different course remains even today a possibility that few are willing to contemplate seriously. After all, as George H. W. Bush declared in 1992, "The American way of life is not negotiable." With nothing negotiable, dependency bred further dependency that took new and virulent forms. Each of Reagan's successors relied increasingly on military power to sustain that way of life. The unspoken assumption has been that profligate spending on what politicians euphemistically refer to as "defense" can sustain profligate domestic consumption of energy and imported manufactures. Unprecedented military might could defer the day of reckoning indefinitely—so at least the hope went.

The munificence of Reagan's military expenditures in the 1980s created untold opportunities to test this proposition. First the elder Bush, then Bill Clinton, and finally the younger Bush wasted no time in exploiting those opportunities, even as it became ever more difficult to justify any of the military operations mounted under their direction as "defensive." Despite Reagan's assurances, by the end of the twentieth century, the United States did, in fact, "start fights" and seemed well on its way to making that something of a national specialty.

By the time the elder George Bush replaced Reagan in

January 1989, Saddam Hussein's usefulness to the United
States had already diminished. When Saddam sent his army
into Kuwait in August 1990 to snatch that country's oil
wealth, he forfeited what little value he still retained in
Washington's eyes.

The result was Operation Desert Storm. Not since 1898,
when Commodore George Dewey's squadron destroyed the
Spanish fleet anchored in Manila Bay, have U.S. forces won
such an ostensibly historic victory that yielded such ironic
results.

Dewey's celebrated triumph gained him passing fame
but accomplished little apart from paving the way for the
United States to annex the Philippines, a strategic gaffe of
the first order. By prevailing in the "Mother of All Battles,"
Desert Storm commander General H. Norman Schwarzkopf
repeated Dewey's achievement. He, too, won momentary
celebrity. On closer examination, however, his feat turned
out to be a good deal less sparkling than advertised. Rather
than serving as a definitive expression of U.S. military
superiority—a show-them-who's-boss moment—Operation
Desert Storm only produced new complications and commitments.

One consequence of "victory" took the form of a large,
permanent, and problematic U.S. military presence in the
Persian Gulf, intended to keep Saddam in his "box" and to
reassure regional allies. Before Operation Desert Storm, the
United States had stationed few troops in the Gulf area, preferring to keep its forces "over the horizon." After Desert
Storm, the United States became, in the eyes of many Muslims at least, an occupying force. The presence of U.S. troops
in Saudi Arabia, site of Islam's holiest shrines, became a
source of particular consternation. As had been the case
with Commodore Dewey, Schwarzkopf's victory turned out

to be neither as clear-cut nor as cheaply won as it first appeared. On the surface, the U.S. position in the wake of Operation Desert Storm seemed unassailable. In actuality, it was precarious.

In January 1993, President Bill Clinton inherited this situation. To his credit, alone among recent presidents Clinton managed at least on occasion to balance the federal budget. With his enthusiasm for globalization, however, the forty-second president exacerbated the underlying contradictions of the American economy. Oil imports increased by more than 50 percent during the Clinton era.[33] The trade imbalance nearly quadrupled.[34] Gross federal debt climbed by nearly $1.5 trillion.[35] During the go-go dot.com years, however, few Americans attended to such matters.

In the Persian Gulf, Clinton's efforts to shore up U.S. hegemony took the form of a "dual containment" policy targeting both Iran and Iraq. With regard to Iran, containment meant further isolating the Islamic republic diplomatically and economically in order to prevent the rebuilding of its badly depleted military forces. With regard to Saddam Hussein's Iraq, it meant much the same, including fierce UN sanctions and a program of armed harassment.

During the first year of his administration, Clinton developed a prodigious appetite for bombing and, thanks to a humiliating "Blackhawk down" failure in and retreat from Somalia, an equally sharp aversion to committing ground troops. Nowhere did Clinton's infatuation with air power find greater application than in Iraq, which he periodically pummeled with precision-guided bombs and cruise missiles. In effect, the cease-fire that terminated Operation Desert Storm in February 1991 did not end the Persian Gulf War. After a brief pause, hostilities resumed. Over time, they intensified, with the United States conducting punitive air strikes at will.

Although when it came to expending the lives of American soldiers, Clinton proved to be circumspect, he expended ordnance with abandon. During the course of his presidency, the navy and air force conducted tens of thousands of sorties into Iraqi airspace, dropped thousands of bombs, and launched hundreds of cruise missiles. Apart from turning various Iraqi military and government facilities into rubble, this cascade of pricy munitions had negligible impact. With American forces suffering not a single casualty, few Americans paid attention to what the ordnance cost or where it landed. After all, whatever the number of bombs dropped, more were always available in a seemingly inexhaustible supply.

Despite these exertions, many in Washington—Republicans and Democrats, politicians and pundits—worked themselves into a frenzy over the fact that Saddam Hussein had managed to survive, when the World's Only Superpower now wished him gone. To fevered minds, Saddam's defiance made him an existential threat, his mere survival an unendurable insult.

In 1998, the anti-Saddam lobby engineered passage through Congress of the Iraq Liberation Act, declaring it "the policy of the United States to seek to remove the Saddam Hussein regime from power in Iraq and to replace it with a democratic government." The legislation, passed unanimously in the Senate and by a 360–38 majority in the House, authorized that the princely sum of $100 million be dedicated to that objective. On October 31, President Clinton duly signed the act into law and issued a statement embracing the cause of freedom for all Iraqis. "I categorically reject arguments that this is unattainable due to Iraq's history or its ethnic or sectarian make-up," the president said. "Iraqis deserve and desire freedom like everyone else."

All of this—both the gratuitous air war and the preposterously frivolous legislation—amounted to theater. Reality on the ground was another matter. A crushing sanctions regime authorized by the UN, but imposed by the United States and its allies, complicated Saddam's life and limited the funds available from Iraqi oil, but primarily had the effect of making the wretched existence of the average Iraqi more wretched still. A 1996 UNICEF report estimated that up to half a million Iraqi children had died as a result of the sanctions. Asked to comment, U.S. Ambassador to the United Nations Madeleine Albright did not even question the figure. Instead, she replied, "I think this is a very hard choice, but the price—we think the price is worth it."

No doubt Albright regretted her obtuse remark. Yet it captured something essential about U.S. policy in the Persian Gulf at a time when confidence in American power had reached its acme. In effect, the United States had forged a partnership with Saddam in imposing massive suffering on the Iraqi people. Yet as long as Americans at home were experiencing a decade of plenty—during the Clinton era, consumers enjoyed low gas prices and gorged themselves on cheap Asian imports—the price that others might be paying didn't much matter.

Bill Clinton's Iraq policy was both strategically misguided and morally indefensible—as ill-advised as John Kennedy's campaign of subversion and sabotage directed against Cuba in the 1960s, as reprehensible as Richard Nixon's illegal bombing of Laos and Cambodia in the late 1960s and 1970s. Yet unlike those actions, which occurred in secret, U.S. policy toward Iraq in the 1990s unfolded in full view of the American people. To say that the policy commanded enthusiastic popular support would be to grossly overstate the case. Yet few Americans strenuously objected—to the bombing, to congressional posturing, or to the brutal sanctions. Paying next to no attention, the great majority quietly acquiesced and thus became complicit.

American Freedom, Iraqi Freedom

To the extent that Bill Clinton's principal critics had a problem with his Iraq policy, their chief complaint was that the United States wasn't dropping enough bombs. Committed to their own quantitative solutions, hawkish conservatives wanted to ratchet up the level of violence. If Saddam's survival represented an affront to American hegemony in the Gulf, then Saddam's elimination offered the necessary corrective. Among neo-Reaganite Republicans, well before 9/11, it became an article of faith that, with Saddam's removal, everything was certain to fall into place. Writing in the *Weekly Standard* in February 1998, Robert Kagan, a leading neoconservative, urged a full-scale invasion. Eliminating the Baath Party regime, he promised, was sure to "open the way for a new post-Saddam Iraq whose intentions can safely be assumed to be benign."[36]

The possibility that military escalation might actually exacerbate America's Persian Gulf dilemma received scant consideration. That the citizens of the United States might ease that dilemma by modifying their own behavior—that the antidote to our ailments might lie within rather than on the other side of the world—received no consideration at all.

The events of September 11, 2001, only hardened this disposition. Among hawks, 9/11 reinforced the conviction that dominance in the Gulf was a categorical imperative. Secretary of Defense Donald Rumsfeld aptly summarized the prevailing view in October 2001: "We have two choices. Either we change the way we live, or we must change the way they live. We choose the latter."[37] If, today, this black-and-white perspective seems a trifle oversimplified, between 2002 and 2004, no politician of national stature had the wit or the gumption to voice a contrary view.[38]

As it trained its sights on modifying the way "they" lived, the Bush administration looked to America's armed forces as its preferred agent of change. The United States would, as Bush and his chief advisers saw it, solidify its hold on the Persian Gulf by relying in the first instance on coercion. In 1991, the president's father had shrunk from doing what they now believed needed to be done: marching on Baghdad and "decapitating" the regime of Saddam Hussein. Throughout the remainder of that decade Clinton had temporized. Now the gloves were coming off, with Saddam's Iraq the primary, but by no means the final, target.

Through a war of liberation, the United States intended to convert Iraq into what Deputy Secretary of Defense Paul Wolfowitz termed "the first Arab democracy."[39] Yet, as they prepared for a final showdown with Saddam, Wolfowitz and others in the administration were already looking beyond Baghdad. In their eyes, Iraq only qualified as an interim objective, a mere way station in a vastly more ambitious enterprise. Baghdad was not Berlin in 1945; it was Warsaw circa 1939.

The ultimate purpose of that exercise was to transform a huge swath of the Islamic world stretching from Morocco all the way through Pakistan and Central Asia to Indonesia and the southern Philippines. Writing in the *New York Times* on October 9, 2002, the journalist Mark Danner got it exactly right. The strategy devised by the Bush administration in response to 9/11 was "comprehensive, prophetic, [and] evangelical." It derived from the assumption that, "for the evils of terror to be defeated," most of the Islamic world needed to "be made new." The ultimate aim of that strategy was nothing less than "to remake the world" or at least what the administration referred to as the Greater Middle East.[40]

Here was an imperial vision on a truly colossal scale, a worthy successor to older claims of "manifest destiny" or of an American mission to "make the world safe for democracy." President Bush's "freedom agenda" updated and expanded upon this tradition.

One might have thought that implementing such a vision would require sustained and large-scale national commitment. Yet soon after 9/11, the American people went back to business as usual—urged to do so by the president himself. "War costs money," Franklin D. Roosevelt had reminded his countrymen after Pearl Harbor. "That means taxes and bonds and bonds and taxes. It means cutting luxuries and other non-essentials."[41] At the outset of its war on terrorism, the Bush administration saw things differently. Even as the United States embarked on a global conflict expected to last decades, the president made a point of reducing taxes. Rather than asking Americans to trim their appetite for luxuries, he called on them to carry on as if nothing had occurred. Barely two weeks after the World Trade Center had collapsed, the president was prodding his fellow citizens to "Get on board. Do your business around the country. Fly and enjoy America's great destination spots. Get down to Disney World in Florida."

Ever so briefly, the events of 9/11 had disrupted American patterns of spending: In the immediate aftermath of September 11, people weren't flocking to Disney World, and airlines seemed to be sliding into bankruptcy. This sudden reticence threatened to bring the empire of consumption crashing down. Hence the urgency of the president's charge to "Take your families and enjoy life, the way we want it to be enjoyed." The theme became one to which the president repeatedly returned. As late as December 2006, with the situation in Iraq looking grim, the wartime president was still exhorting his countrymen not to curb their appetites but to indulge them. Bush noted with satisfaction that the nation's annual holiday season spending binge was off to "a strong beginning." Yet the president summoned Americans to make even greater exertions: "I encourage you all to go shopping more."

Previously, war had implied some requirement to do without or at least to tighten belts. During World War II, rationing had caused modest discomfort, not real distress, but at least Americans on the home front faced daily reminders that there was a war on. In President Bush's war, the role allotted to the American people was to pretend that the conflict did not exist. Despite claims that his would be a generational struggle, the president never considered restoring the draft. Nor did he bother to expand the size of the armed forces. This guaranteed that the 0.5 percent of the population that made up the all-volunteer force would bear the brunt of any sacrifice. With only a handful of dissenters, the remaining 99.5 percent of Americans happily endorsed this distribution of effort.

Predictably, as the scope of military operations grew, especially after the invasion of Iraq in March 2003, so too did the level of military spending. During the Bush years, the Pentagon's annual budget more than doubled, reaching $700 billion by 2008. This time, unlike in Operation Desert Storm when Germany, Japan, and friendly Gulf states ponied up tens of billions of dollars to defray the cost of U.S. operations, the burden of paying for the war fell entirely on Washington.

Less predictably, although perhaps not surprisingly, spending on entitlements also rose in the years after 9/11. Abetted by Congress, the Bush administration conducted a war of guns *and* butter, including huge increases in outlays for Medicare and Social Security. The federal budget once more went into the red and stayed there.

In the name of preserving the American way of life, President Bush and his lieutenants committed the nation to a breathtakingly ambitious project of near global domination. Hewing to a tradition that extended at least as far back as Jefferson, they intended to expand American power to further the cause of American freedom. Freedom assumed abundance. Abundance seemingly required access to large quantities of cheap oil. Guaranteeing access to that oil demanded that the United States remove all doubts about who called the shots in the Persian Gulf. It demanded oil wars.

Yet that way of life, based for at least two generations on an ethic of self-gratification and excess, drastically reduced the resources available for such an all-encompassing imperial enterprise. Encouraged by President Bush to attend to their personal priorities, Americans lost no time disengaging themselves from the war he had launched. Most remained spectators, rather than even marginal participants. Bush and others in his administration repeatedly declared that the United States was a "nation at war." Washington may have fancied itself to be at war; the nation most assuredly was not.

While soldiers fought, people consumed. With the United States possessing less than 3 percent of the world's known oil reserves and Americans burning one out of every four barrels of petroleum produced worldwide, oil imports reached 60 percent of daily national requirements and kept rising.[42] The personal savings rate continued to plummet. In 2005, it dropped below zero and remained there. Collectively, Americans were now spending more than they earned.[43] By 2006, the annual trade imbalance reached a whopping $818 billion.[44] The following year, total public debt topped $9 trillion, or nearly 70 percent of the gross national product.[45]

Many Americans were indeed enjoying life the way it was meant to be enjoyed, at least as enjoyment had come to be defined in the first years of the twenty-first century. In February 2006, a provocative article in the *New York Times Magazine* posed the question "Is freedom just another word for many things to buy?"[46] Through their actions after 9/11, as before, tens of millions of Americans answered in the affirmative.

Given the extent to which a penchant for consumption had become the driveshaft of the global economy, the Bush administration welcomed the average citizen's inclination to ignore the war and return to the shopping mall. Yet once the Iraq War demonstrated the shortcomings of shock-and-awe, there was no obvious way to reconfigure the empire of consumption into an empire of global liberation. In post-9/11 America, the young men and women rallying to the colors never reached more than a trickle. Few parents were eager to offer up their sons and daughters to fight Bush's war. The horrors of September 11 notwithstanding, most Americans subscribed to a limited-liability version of patriotism, one that emphasized the display of bumper stickers in preference to shouldering a rucksack.

Had the administration gotten a quick win in Iraq, it might have finessed the crisis of profligacy—for a while. To put it mildly, however, the war didn't follow its assigned script.

Between April 28, 2003, and February 22, 2006, Iraq came apart at the seams. During this interval, the adverse foreign policy implications of American profligacy became indisputable. On the former date, skittish American soldiers in Fallujah fired into a crowd of demonstrators, killing a dozen or more Iraqis. If the insurgency had a trigger, this was it.

On the latter date, terrorists blew up the Mosque of the Golden Dome in Samarra, igniting an already simmering Sunni-Shiite civil war. Prior to the incident in Fallujah, the administration could still convince itself that its grand strategy remained plausible. Even a month later, swaggering White House officials were still bragging: "Anyone can go to Baghdad. Real men go to Tehran." By the time the Samarra bombing occurred, events had not dealt kindly with such fantasies. Real men were holed up in Baghdad's heavily fortified Green Zone.

As conditions in Iraq worsened, the disparity between pretensions and capacities became painfully evident. A generation of profligacy had produced strategic insolvency. The administration had counted on the qualitative superiority of U.S. forces compensating for their limited numbers. The enemy did not cooperate.

Although the United States is a wealthy nation with a population of over 300 million, closing the gap between means and ends posed a daunting task. By February 2005, this was so apparent that *Los Angeles Times* columnist Max Boot was suggesting that the armed forces "open up recruiting stations from Budapest to Bangkok, Cape Town to Cairo, Montreal to Mexico City." Boot's suggestion that the Bush administration raise up a "Freedom Legion" of foreign mercenaries inadvertently illustrated the depth of the problem.[47] If the Pentagon needed to comb the streets of Cape Town and Cairo to fill its ranks, the situation was indeed dire.

The United States had a shortage of soldiers; it also lacked funds. The longer the wars in Iraq and Afghanistan dragged on, the more costly they became. By 2007, to sustain its operations, the U.S. command in Baghdad was burning through $3 billion per week. That same year, the overall costs of the Iraq War topped the $500-billion mark, with some estimates already suggesting that the final bill could reach at least $2 trillion.[48]

Although these figures were widely reported, they had almost no political impact in Washington, indicating the extent to which habits of profligacy had become entrenched. Congress responded to budget imbalances not by trimming spending or increasing revenues but by quietly and repeatedly raising the debt ceiling—by $3.015 trillion between 2002 and 2006.[49] Future generations could figure out how to pay the bills.

All this red ink generated nervous speculation about a coming economic collapse comparable in magnitude to the Great Depression.[50] Whatever the merit of such concerns, the interest here is not in what may yet happen to the American economy but in what has already occurred to its foreign policy.

By 2007, the United States was running out of troops and was already out of money. According to conventional wisdom, when it came to Iraq, there were "no good options." Yet Americans had limited the range of possible options by their stubborn insistence that the remedy to the nation's problems in the Persian Gulf necessarily lay in the Persian Gulf rather than at home. The slightest suggestion that the United States ought to worry less about matters abroad and more about setting its own house in order elicited from the political elite, Republicans and Democrats alike, shrieks of "isolationism," the great imaginary sin to which Americans are allegedly prone. Yet to begin to put our house in order would be to open up a whole new array of options, once again permitting the United States to "choose peace or war, as our interest, guided by justice, shall counsel."

Long accustomed to thinking of the United States as a superpower, Americans have yet to realize that they have forfeited command of their own destiny. The reciprocal relationship between expansionism, abundance, and freedom—each reinforcing the other—no longer exists. If anything, the reverse is true: Expansionism squanders American wealth and power, while putting freedom at risk. As a consequence, the strategic tradition to which Jefferson and Polk, Lincoln and McKinley, TR and FDR all subscribed has been rendered not only obsolete but pernicious.

Rather than confronting this reality head-on, American grand strategy since the era of Ronald Reagan, and especially throughout the era of George W. Bush, has been characterized by attempts to wish reality away. Policy makers have been engaged in a de facto Ponzi scheme intended to extend indefinitely the American line of credit. The fiasco of the Iraq War and the quasi-permanent U.S. occupation of Afghanistan illustrate the results and prefigure what is yet to come if the crisis of American profligacy continues unabated.

2. The Political Crisis

In the summer of 1940, Franklin D. Roosevelt began mobilizing the United States for total war. In the spring of 1947, a mere eighteen months after VJ Day, Harry S Truman inaugurated a series of steps that returned the nation to a war footing. There matters would stand for decades to come.

Together, these successive mobilizations—the first for World War II, the latter for the Cold War—overturned America's traditional political system and replaced it with something quite new. FDR's predecessors had presided over a republic. Central to the functioning of that republic was a set of checks and balances designed to limit the concentration of political power. Truman's successors presided over a system *defined by* the concentration of power, both in Washington and, within Washington, in the executive branch. To describe the result as a republic is to misconstrue the essential nature of the thing, like calling Adolf Hitler a dictator or the weapon dropped on Hiroshima a bomb.

In contemporary American politics, appearances belie reality. Although the text of the Constitution has changed but little since FDR's day, the actual system of governance conceived by the framers—a federal republic deriving its authority from the people in which the central government exercises limited and specified powers—no longer pertains. Citizens disgusted with what many see as a perpetual mess in Washington yearn for a restoration of a mythical Old Republic. Yet one might as well hope for the revival of the family farm or for physicians to resume making house calls.

According to Niebuhr, "The democratic techniques of a free society place checks upon the power of the ruler and administrator and thus prevent it from becoming vexatious."[1] To the extent that this offers an apt definition of democracy, then, American democracy in our time has suffered notable decay. Checks upon the power exercised by the ruler have eroded badly, with frequently vexing results.

Since 1940, a succession of national security emergencies, real and imagined, have permitted the federal government to assume a vast array of new responsibilities at the expense of state and local authorities.[2] In tandem with this shift and helped mightily by an atmosphere of seemingly permanent crisis, the presidency has amassed greatly expanded prerogatives. Beginning with the election of John F. Kennedy in 1960, the occupant of the White House has become a combination of demigod, father figure, and, inevitably, the betrayer of inflated hopes. Pope, pop star, scold, scapegoat, crisis manager, commander in chief, agenda setter, moral philosopher, interpreter of the nation's charisma, object of veneration, and the butt of jokes—regardless of personal attributes and qualifications, the president is perforce all these rolled into one.

Critics of whoever happens to occupy the White House

often make a show of decrying the resulting "imperial presidency." This qualifies as mere posturing. In fact, for members of the political class, serving, gaining access to, reporting
on, second-guessing, or gossiping about the emperor-
president (or about those aspiring to succeed him) has become an abiding preoccupation.

The imperial presidency would not exist were it not for
the Congress, which has willingly ceded authority to the executive branch, especially on matters touching, however remotely, on national security. As the chief executive achieved
supremacy, the legislative branch not only lost clout but grad-
ually made itself the object of ridicule. David Addington,
chief of staff to Vice President Dick Cheney, pungently described the philosophy of the Bush administration this way:
"We're going to push and push and push until some larger
force makes us stop."[3] Even under Democratic control, the
Congress has not remotely threatened to be that larger force.

No one today seriously believes that the actions of the
legislative branch are informed by a collective determination to promote the common good. For this very reason, periodic congressional efforts to curb abuses of presidential
power are mostly for show and mostly inspired by a desire
to gain some partisan advantage.

The chief remaining function of Congress is to ensure
the reelection of its members, best achieved by shameless
gerrymandering, doling out prodigious amounts of political
pork, and seeing to the protection of certain vested interests. Testifying to the spectacular effectiveness of these techniques, in 2006, 93 percent of senators and representatives
running for reelection won.[4] The United States has become a
de facto one-party state, with the legislative branch permanently controlled by an Incumbents' Party.

Although relatively few legislators are overtly dishonest,

in the sense of taking bribes or kickbacks, a subtler form of corruption pervades both the Senate and the House of Representatives. The Congress may not be a den of iniquity, but it is a haven for narcissistic hacks, for whom self-promotion and self-preservation take precedence over serious engagement with serious issues.

To judge by the impassioned rhetoric heard on Capitol Hill, one might think otherwise. Yet even as they take turns denouncing one another, the two parties tacitly collaborate to maintain a status quo that both find eminently satisfactory. To be sure, party loyalists and ideologues of various stripes maintain the pretense that issues of decisive importance are at stake. Right-wingers charge tax-and-spend liberals with being socialists or worse. Self-styled progressives accuse conservatives of conspiring to send women into back alleys to end unwanted pregnancies. But this amounts to little more than theater.

To provide a specific and execrable illustration of politics-as-theater, one need look no farther than the actions of the Democratic Party in relation to Iraq. Midterm elections in November 2006, widely seen as a referendum on the war, created a Democratic majority in both houses of Congress. The new Senate majority leader Harry Reid and the new Speaker of the House Nancy Pelosi claimed that their party had a mandate to change course. "The American people made clear in last fall's election," Pelosi announced in early 2007, that "they want a new direction on Iraq." She promised "tough accountability leading to the responsible redeployment of our troops."[5]

Yet such promises proved to be empty. Although Reid and Pelosi routinely denounced the war as misbegotten and misguided, their commitment to forcing a change in policy took a backseat to their concern to protect the Democratic majority. A real showdown with the White House over war funding could have placed that majority at risk. So President Bush got the money he wanted. The war that Americans had elected Democrats to shut down continued. The referendum of November 2006 hadn't mattered.

The rise of the imperial presidency and the demise of the Congress as a coequal branch of government have produced periodic bouts of hand-wringing. Practically speaking, however, these constitutional deformities might not matter much if the result were an effective system of governance— if, that is, an apparatus dominated by an imperial presidency performed the several functions laid out in the Preamble of the Constitution and did so in a timely and affordable fashion.

But here lies the rub. The chief attribute of the actually existing system—all of the institutions, structures, and arrangements implied by the word *Washington*—is dysfunction. As the federal city emerged as the center of American power, it was occupied by a gang that couldn't shoot straight. Regardless of which party is in power, the people in charge don't know what they are doing. As a consequence, policies devised by Washington tend to be extravagant, wasteful, ill-conceived, misguided, unsuccessful, or simply beside the point. To cite examples drawn from just the past several years, think of the bungled efforts to "reform" the Social Security and health-care systems or to fix immigration policy. Think of the inanity of the never-ending "war on drugs." Think of the ill-starred federal response to Hurricane Katrina.

The problem with the existing system of government is not that it differs from what the authors of the Federalist Papers intended or from what elementary school students learn about in social studies. The problem is that what we have doesn't work. The gross incompetence of those who preside over the federal apparatus is appalling and unacceptable.

Washington ought to symbolize enlightened governance. Instead, a system conceived "to form a more perfect Union, establish Justice, insure domestic Tranquility, provide for the common defense, promote the general Welfare, and secure the Blessings of Liberty to ourselves and our Posterity" poses a clear and present danger to those it is meant to serve. This is the political crisis confronting Americans today.

The Ideology of National Security

The ineptitude of the federal government is especially acute when it comes to national security—the very issue that, since 1940, has provided the chief rationale for finishing off the Old Republic. The national security state that evolved during World War II and through the long decades of the Cold War endangers the nation it was created to protect. It undermines rather than enhances security. To substantiate that judgment, one need only recall the events of the present decade, including the failure to anticipate and avert 9/11; the failure to bring to justice its chief architects; the failure to devise a realistic and strategically coherent response to the threat posed by Islamic extremism; and above all the egregious failures associated with the Iraq and Afghan wars.

Any one of these four failures ought to raise serious questions about the competence of those charged with responsibility for the nation's security. That all four should have occurred in half the span of a single decade surely constitutes something akin to a definitive judgment. Granted, everyone makes mistakes. Nobody bats a thousand. To err is human. Yet these familiar rationalizations simply won't do. Some mistakes, even honest ones, cannot be forgiven. The record of miscalculation and misfeasance that is the narrative of national security policy since 2001 extends orders of magnitude beyond inexcusable.

Critics intent on assigning blame for this hapless record have offered three explanations. The first holds President Bush personally responsible, charging him with combining in his person a rare mix of hubris and recklessness fueled by personal religiosity. The second broadens the charge to include a rogue's gallery of nefarious lieutenants like Vice President Dick Cheney, former Secretary of Defense Donald Rumsfeld, and the president's former "brain," political strategist Karl Rove. The third explanation broadens the charge further still to include a cabal of neoconservatives said to exercise diabolical influence over the president and his inner circle. Implicit in all three of these views is the assumption that a different chief executive with different advisers open to advice and counsel from a different quarter—the Brookings Institution, say, rather than the American Enterprise Institute, the *New Republic* rather than the *Weekly Standard*—would have followed a different course and achieved notably better results.

There is a fourth possibility. This explanation begins with the acknowledgment that the Bush administration did not create the problems that came home to roost on September 11, 2001. It inherited them. Without question, Bush's actions served to make things worse. Yet even though his response to 9/11 did contain some innovative features—most prominently, the misguided Bush Doctrine of preventive war—the president has for the most part operated within the framework that has defined basic national security policy for decades.

To state the matter directly: Observers preoccupied with delineating the differences between this Republican president and that Democratic one may uncover any number of small truths while missing the big ones. Identifying the big truths requires an appreciation for continuity rather than change. It's not the superficial distinctions that matter but the subterranean similarities.

President Bush's critics and his dwindling band of loyalists share this conviction: that the forty-third president has broken decisively with the past, setting the United States on a revolutionary new course. Yet this is poppycock. The truth is this: Bush and those around him have reaffirmed the pre-existing fundamentals of U.S. policy, above all affirming the ideology of national security to which past administrations have long subscribed. Bush's main achievement has been to articulate that ideology with such fervor and clarity as to unmask as never before its defects and utter perversity.

Four core convictions inform this ideology of national security. In his second inaugural address, President Bush testified eloquently to each of them.

According to the first of these convictions, history has an identifiable and indisputable purpose. History, the president declared, "has a visible direction, set by liberty and the Author of Liberty." History's abiding theme is freedom, to which all humanity aspires. Reduced to its essentials, history is an epic struggle, binary in nature, between "oppression, which is always wrong, and freedom, which is eternally right."

According to the second conviction, the United States has always embodied, and continues to embody, freedom. America has always been, and remains, freedom's chief exemplar and advocate. "From the day of our Founding," the president said, "we have proclaimed that every man and woman on this earth has rights, and dignity, and matchless value, because they bear the image of the Maker of Heaven and earth." As the self-proclaimed Land of Liberty, the United States serves as the vanguard of history. Revising, refining, and perfecting their understanding of freedom,

Americans constantly model its meaning for others around the world. In 1839, the journalist John L. O'Sullivan described the young United States as "the Great Nation of Futurity." So it remains today. Within the confines of the United States, history's intentions are most fully revealed.

According to the third conviction, Providence summons America to ensure freedom's ultimate triumph. This, observed President Bush, "is the mission that created our Nation." The Author of Liberty has anointed the United States as the Agent of Liberty. Unique among great powers, this nation pursues interests larger than itself. When it acts, it does so on freedom's behalf and at the behest of higher authority. By invading Iraq, the United States reaffirmed and reinvigorated the nation's "great liberating tradition," as the president put it. In so doing, "we have lit a fire as well—a fire in the minds of men. It warms those who feel its power, it burns those who fight its progress, and one day this untamed fire of freedom will reach the darkest corners of our world." Only cynics or those disposed toward evil could possibly dissent from this self-evident truth.

According to the final conviction, for the American way of life to endure, freedom must prevail everywhere. Only when the light of freedom's untamed fire illuminates the world's darkest corners will America's own safety and prosperity be assured. Or as the president expressed it, "The survival of liberty in our land increasingly depends on the success of liberty in other lands." In effect, what the United States offers to the world and what it requires of the world align precisely. Put simply, "America's vital interests and our deepest beliefs are now one." This proposition serves, of course, as an infinitely expansible grant of authority, empowering the United States to assert its influence anywhere it chooses since, by definition, it acts on freedom's behalf.

This line of thinking comes with a rich and ancient

pedigree. We can trace its origins back to 1630, when John Winthrop enjoined the first white settlers of Massachusetts Bay to erect a "city upon a hill," or to 1776, when Tom Paine declared that it lay within America's power "to begin the world over again"—sentiments, as we have noted, that Ronald Reagan skillfully resurrected. Time and again during America's ascent to power, variants of this ideology provided the impetus for expansionism. Appearing in 1846 under the guise of Manifest Destiny, it lent moral cover to James Polk's efforts to secure the lebensraum Americans coveted. In 1898, urgent calls to "liberate" nearby Cuba nudged William McKinley into a war that ended with the United States in possession of a maritime empire that extended all the way to the western Pacific.

Yet only since World War II has this ideology established itself as the fixed backdrop for policy. Indeed, it derives much of its persuasive power from the way that Americans remember that war, converting the events of the 1930s and 1940s into a parable of universal significance. Hence the inclination to portray almost any heavy not to Washington's liking as another Adolf Hitler or Joseph Stalin, with the failure to confront that adversary as tantamount to "appeasement" and with nothing less than the survival of civilization itself at stake.

At a time when pundits and policy makers routinely liken the threat of Islamic radicalism to the threat posed by the totalitarianisms of the last century, it is worth recalling that U.S. officials once compared the totalitarians to historic Islam. "The threat to Western Europe," wrote Truman's secretary of state, Dean Acheson, in his memoirs, "seemed to me singularly like that which Islam had posed centuries before, with its combination of ideological zeal and fighting power."[6] Treating Nazism, communism, and Islamism as essentially interchangeable, while ignoring their fundamental and irreconcilable differences, testifies to the enduring value of using (or devising) some sort of diabolical "other" as a reference point when selling policy. In Acheson's day, comparing communists to fanatical Muslims left little room for doubt about the seriousness of the Red threat. Today, comparing Islamic extremists to fanatical communists or, even worse, to Nazis accomplishes a similar purpose. The intention is to simplify, clarify, and remove ambiguity. The net effect is to mobilize, discipline, and squelch dissent.

The ideology of national security does not serve as an operational checklist. It imposes no specific obligations. It functions the way ideology so often does—not to divine truth or even to make sense of things, but to provide a highly elastic rationale for action. In the American context, it serves principally to legitimate the exercise of executive power. It removes constraints, conferring upon presidents and their immediate circle of advisers wide prerogatives for deciding when and how to employ that power.

Nothing about this ideology, however, mandates action in support of the ideals it celebrates. It doesn't, for example, oblige the United States to do anything on behalf of the people of Zimbabwe or Burma, no matter how heavy the yoke of oppression they are obliged to bear. It certainly does not prevent American policy makers from collaborating with debased authoritarian regimes that deny basic freedoms like Hosni Mubarak's Egypt or Pervez Musharraf's Pakistan. What it does do is provide policy makers with a moral gloss that can be added to virtually any initiative by insisting that, whatever concrete interests might be at stake, the United States is also acting to advance the cause of freedom and democracy.

Postwar presidents have routinely tapped elements of

this ideology as a source of authority. America's status as a force for good in a world that pits good against evil has provided a rationale for bribing foreign officials, assassinating foreign leaders, overthrowing governments, and undertaking major military interventions. George W. Bush did not invent this practice; he merely inherited and expanded upon it.

Through constant repetition, the elements of this ideology have become hardwired into the American psyche. They function as articles of faith, beyond question and beyond scrutiny. Do politicians like Bush, who habitually cite the tenets of this faith, genuinely believe what they are saying? In all likelihood they do, just as Fox News anchors may genuinely believe that they provide "fair and balanced" coverage of world affairs, just as McDonald's franchisees may genuinely believe that theirs is a business of "serving up smiles." Conviction follows self-interest.

Aspirants to high office likewise testify to the core tenets of this ideology, hoping thereby to demonstrate their essential trustworthiness. Here is the version offered in December 1991 by the then-governor of Arkansas, a liberal Democrat whose foreign policy credentials were nonexistent but who had his sights trained on the White House.

> I was born nearly a half-century ago, at the dawn of the Cold War, a time of great change, enormous opportunity, and uncertain peril. At a time when Americans wanted nothing more than to come home and resume their lives of peace and quiet, our country had to summon the will for a new kind of war— containing an expansionist and hostile Soviet Union which vowed to bury us. We had to find ways to rebuild the economies of Europe and Asia, encourage a worldwide movement toward independence, and vindicate our nation's principles in the world against

yet another totalitarian challenge to liberal democracy. Thanks to the unstinting courage and sacrifice of the American people, we were able to win that Cold War.[7]

This was a rendering of history with all the details air-brushed away—no allusions to Vietnam, no reference to CIA coups and attempted assassinations, no mention of collaborating with venal autocrats like Cuba's Fulgencio Batista, Nicaragua's Anastasio Somoza Debayle, or the Philippines' Ferdinand Marcos. Yet the passage served Bill Clinton's purposes precisely, allowing him to situate himself well within the American political mainstream. Clinton understood, quite correctly, that were he to stray too far from that mainstream—as, for example, presidential candidate George McGovern did in the presidential campaign of 1972 when he summoned America to "come home"—he would doom his candidacy. Although Clinton himself had done absolutely nothing to win the Cold War—he had actually labored mightily and successfully to avoid military service—through his repeated use of the term *we* he established his personal identification with that struggle. He was one with "us," and "we" had prevailed in a historic contest, thereby gaining a great victory for freedom.

Fast-forward sixteen years, and another would-be president with sketchy foreign policy credentials unhesitatingly ripped a page out of the Clinton playbook. "At moments of great peril in the last century," declared Senator Barack Obama,

American leaders such as Franklin Roosevelt, Harry Truman, and John F. Kennedy managed both to protect the American people and to expand opportunity for the next generation. What is more, they ensured that America, by deed and example, led and lifted

the world—that we stood for and fought for the freedoms sought by billions of people beyond our borders.

As Roosevelt built the most formidable military
the world had ever seen, his Four Freedoms gave purpose to our struggle against fascism. Truman cham-
pioned a bold new architecture to respond to the
Soviet threat—one that paired military strength with
the Marshall Plan and helped secure the peace and
well-being of nations around the world.

Like Clinton, Obama was intent on identifying himself
with the cause that "we stood for and fought for." Like Clinton, in recounting the heroic narrative in which Roosevelt,
Truman, and their successors had figured so prominently,
he was testifying to that narrative's essential truth and continuing validity.

Yet almost inescapably he also subscribed to George W.
Bush's own interpretation of that narrative. As Obama went
on to explain, "The security and well-being of each and
every American depend on the security and well-being of
those who live beyond our borders." Like Bush—like those
who had preceded Bush—Obama defined America's purposes in cosmic terms. "The mission of the United States,"
he proclaimed, "is to provide global leadership grounded in
the understanding that the world shares a common security
and a common humanity."[8]

Clinton's rhetorical sleight of hand, mimicked by
Obama, illustrates the role that the ideology of national security plays in shaping electoral politics. That role is chiefly
to provide a reductive and insipid, if ultimately reassuring,
view of reality. Accept the proposition that America is freedom's tribune, and it becomes a small step to believing that
the "peace process" aims to achieve peace, that Iraq quali-

fies as a sovereign state, and that Providence has summoned the United States to wage an all-out war against "terrorism." Indeed, to disagree with these sentiments—as the Washington consensus sees it—is to stray beyond the bounds of permissible opinion.

Prior to World War II, Niebuhr wrote, "No simple victory of good over evil in history is possible."[9] For Bill Clinton and Barack Obama, as for George W. Bush, the actions of the United States during World War II and ever since refute that claim. Theirs is a usable past in which good eventually triumphs as long as America remains faithful to its mission.

In this way, ideology serves as a device for sharply narrowing the range of policy debate. Dissent, where it exists, seldom penetrates the centers of power in Washington. Principled dissenters, whether paleoconservatives or libertarians, pacifists or neo-agrarians, remain on the political fringes, dismissed as either mean-spirited (that is, unable to appreciate the lofty motives that inform U.S. policy) or simply naive (that is, oblivious to the implacable evil that the United States is called upon to confront).

The ideology of national security persists not because it expresses empirically demonstrable truths but because it serves the interests of those who created the national security state and those who still benefit from its continued existence—the very people who are most responsible for the increasingly maladroit character of U.S. policy.

These are the men, along with a few women, who comprise the self-selecting, self-perpetuating camarilla that, since World War II, has shaped (and perverted) national security policy. In a famous book published over a half century ago, the sociologist C. Wright Mills took a stab at describing this "power elite."[10] His depiction of an interlocking corporate, political, and military directorate remains valid today, although one might amend it to acknowledge the role played by insider journalists and policy intellectuals who serve as propagandists, gatekeepers, and packagers of the latest conventional wisdom. Although analysts employed by the RAND Corporation or the Hudson Institute may not themselves qualify as full-fledged members of the national security elite, they facilitate its functioning. Much the same can be said about columnists who write for the *New York Times*, the *Washington Post*, or the *Weekly Standard*, the research fellows busily organizing study groups at the Council on Foreign Relations or the American Enterprise Institute, and the policy-oriented academics who inhabit institutions like Harvard's Kennedy School of Government or Princeton's Wilson School.

To say that a power elite directs the affairs of state is not to suggest the existence of some dark conspiracy. It is simply to acknowledge the way Washington actually works. Especially on matters related to national security, policy making has become oligarchic rather than democratic. The policy-making process is not open but closed, with the voices of privileged insiders carrying unimaginably greater weight than those of the unwashed masses.

According to Mills, the power elite and those trafficking in ideas useful to its core membership share a "cast of mind that defines international reality as basically military."[11] This was true when Mills wrote those words in the 1950s, and it is even truer today. For members of the policy elite, imperfect security is by definition inadequate security. Where gaps exist, they need to be filled. Defenses must be shored up. Yet ultimately, as the writers James Chace and Caleb Carr once observed, absolute security "cannot be negotiated; it can only be won."[12] And winning implies the possession of military might along with a willingness to use it.

In consonance with this "military ascendancy," these American hawks are inclined to see the United States as already beset by acutely dangerous threats, with even greater perils lurking just around the corner. With a low tolerance for uncertainty, they are highly attuned to the putative risks of waiting on events, while discounting the hazards posed by precipitate action. This perspective found classic expression in September 2002, when Condoleezza Rice rejected a lack of detailed intelligence about Iraq's nuclear program as a reason to postpone a planned invasion of that country since "we don't want the smoking gun to be a mushroom cloud." For his part, Vice President Cheney was even more explicit. Even a remotely suspected threat could provide a sufficient rationale for action. "If there's a one percent chance that Pakistani scientists are helping al Qaeda build or develop a nuclear weapon," Cheney once remarked, "we have to treat it as a certainty in terms of our response."[13]

Perceived threats, even when faint, improbable, or (like that Iraqi nuclear program) at worst distant, invariably demand an urgent response, which no less invariably involves enhancing, reconfiguring, deploying, or actually using American coercive power. Long before Rice, Cheney, and others in the Bush administration were seized by the idea that Saddam Hussein's very existence had become unendurable, this mind-set had convinced U.S. policy makers that, in 1953, Iran's prime minister, Mohammad Mossadegh, and, in 1954, Guatemala's president, Jacobo Arbenz Guzman, needed to go, that the Bay of Pigs operation in 1961 and its illegitimate offspring, Operation Mongoose, qualified as good ideas, and that propping up the wobbly dominoes of Southeast Asia during the 1960s constituted a vital interest worth the sacrifice of fifty-eight thousand American lives. In the 1980s, this same mind-set prompted the United States to throw in with Saddam Hussein, President Ronald Reagan's administration having been seized by the idea that Iran's ayatollahs posed a dire threat.

Granted, statecraft makes for strange bedfellows. Realpolitik leaves only limited room for consistency and high-mindedness. Yet from the late 1940s to the present day, members of the power elite have shown an almost pathological tendency to misinterpret reality and inflate threats. The advisers to whom imperial presidents have turned for counsel have specialized not in cool judgment but in frenzied overreaction. Although the hawks have not always prevailed—in 1954, Dwight D. Eisenhower deflected urgings to intervene in French Indochina, and in 1962, John F. Kennedy rejected the advice of those pressing to bomb Soviet military installations in Cuba—more often than not the proponents of action, whether advocating direct intervention, relying on covert means, or working through proxies, have carried the day. The hawks may not always advocate immediate war per se, but they lean forward in the saddle, keeping sabers drawn and at the ready. The mantra of the hawks is the barely veiled threat: "All options remain on the table."

The ideology of national security underwrites a bipartisan consensus that since World War II has lent to foreign policy a remarkable consistency. While it does not prevent criticism of particular policies or policy makers, it robs any debate over policy of real substance.

State of Insecurity

In the present-day political system, the president-emperor functions as the ultimate "decider." Yet, in a complex and rapidly changing world, no president can know all that he needs to know or manage personally the vast array of responsibilities that have accrued to his office. As a consequence, since World War II, Congress and the executive branch have collaborated in creating a large, permanent, and ever-expanding national security apparatus.

Today, everything about the national security state is gargantuan: its payroll, total budget, organizational complexity, appetite for information, ability to churn out reams of self-justifying press releases, and capacity for dissembling, chicanery, and dirty tricks. The Pentagon alone houses a workforce of 25,000 employees, who each day make 200,000 phone calls and send a million e-mails, while occupying 3,705,793 square feet of office space, traipsing 17.5 miles of corridors, mounting 131 staircases, watching 4,200 clocks, drinking from 691 water fountains, and relieving themselves in 284 lavatories.[14]

Although nominally serving the public, the institutions making up this apparatus go to great lengths to evade public scrutiny, performing their duties shielded behind multiple layers of secrecy. Ostensibly, this cult of secrecy exists to deny information to America's enemies. Its actual purpose is to control the information provided to the American people, releasing only what a particular agency or administration is eager to make known, while withholding (or providing in sanitized form) information that might embarrass the government or call into question its policies. In 1961, the social critic Lewis Mumford described the already expansive national security state's modus operandi this way: "one-way communication, the priestly monopoly of secret knowledge, the multiplication of secret agencies, the suppression of open discussion, and even the insulation of error against public criticism and exposure . . . which in practice nullifies public reaction and makes rational dissent the equivalent of patriotic disaffection, if not treason."[15] Events since have affirmed Mumford's view many times over.

The case of *United States v. Reynolds*, 345 U.S. 1 (1953) provides an early, telling illustration of how the system works. In October 1948, a B-29 Superfortress bomber engaged in testing an electronic device crashed near Waycross, Georgia, killing several of those on board. Widows of the deceased crewmen, wanting to know what had caused the crash, petitioned the air force to release the accident investigation report. Air force officials refused, claiming that they could not comply "without seriously hampering national security." When the widows sued, the Supreme Court found in favor of the air force. Writing for the majority, Chief Justice Fred Vinson asserted that in "a time of vigorous preparation for national defense" the courts should steer clear of telling senior national security officials what information to release and what to withhold. Given the overriding importance of keeping secrets absolutely secret, wrote Vinson, courts needed to take officials at their word: "Insisting upon an examination of the evidence, even by the judge alone, in chambers," posed too great a risk.[16]

A half century later, when the Pentagon finally declassified the accident report, it held no sensitive information at all; rather, it showed that the aircraft had crashed due to poor maintenance and pilot error. The air force had used claims of national security to conceal garden-variety organizational ineptitude.[17]

Such behavior is by no means unique to the air force, nor was it peculiar to the early Cold War. For the principal institutions that make up the national security state—the State Department, the armed services, the various intelligence agencies, the Joint Chiefs of Staff, the Office of the Secretary of Defense, the staff of the National Security Council, and the FBI—this has become standard procedure. It would be wrong to charge all of the officials employed by these agencies with engaging in a conscious effort to fleece or abuse the American people. Yet it would not be wrong to suggest that an eagerness to advance institutional interests and protect institutional reputations trumps all other considerations and routinely provides the basis for behavior that is dishonest, unprofessional, unethical, and frequently at odds with the nation's well-being.

The period since 9/11 has produced a plethora of supporting examples. Recall, for instance, the saga of PFC Jessica Lynch, captured by Iraqi forces during the early days of the Iraq War. Although Lynch herself behaved honorably throughout, the Pentagon embellished her ordeal with fraudulent heroics and then transformed her subsequent rescue into a tale of stirring derring-do, most of it wholly imaginary. Then there was the story of army ranger and former NFL football player Pat Tillman. When Tillman lost his life in Afghanistan, his chain of command concocted a fictionalized account of what had happened: There had been a fierce firefight; Tillman had performed with great valor; ultimately, he fell to enemy fire. His commanders hastily awarded Tillman a posthumous Silver Star for gallantry. The result was a triumph of public relations. Yet soon enough, the tale unraveled: The truth turned out to be that Tillman's own comrades had killed him in a friendly-fire incident.

The policy significance of these falsified battle accounts is slight. Still, the calculated exploitation of Jessica Lynch and the effort to mislead Pat Tillman's parents regarding the cause of their son's death do not speak well of an institution that purports to care above all about soldiers and their families. Beyond that, whether we ascribe the Lynch and Tillman episodes to bad judgment, arrogance, or downright stupidity, they are not isolated examples. Since 9/11, national security officials have been complicit in other disinformation campaigns of far greater relevance to policy. These include trumpeting the dangers of nonexistent Iraqi weapons of mass destruction; trivializing the anarchy in Baghdad following the overthrow of Saddam Hussein ("Stuff happens!") and the scope of the insurgency ("pockets of dead-enders"); tagging a handful of low-ranking U.S. enlisted troops with responsibility for the systematic abuse of Iraqi prisoners at Abu Ghraib; and consistently underreporting the civilian casualties caused as a by-product of U.S. military operations in both Iraq and Afghanistan.

No matter how great the disaster—in relation to Iraq alone, consider the flawed intelligence used to justify the invasion, the bungled occupation, and the billions of "reconstruction" dollars squandered or stolen as a result of incompetence or blatant corruption—senior officials operate on the implicit assumption that they are immunized from accountability. In May 2007, in a stinging critique of post-9/11 military leadership, Army Lieutenant Colonel Paul Yingling wrote in *Armed Forces Journal* that "a private who loses a rifle suffers far greater consequences than a general who loses a war."[18] Yingling is correct—and one could easily broaden his indictment to include high-ranking civilians. A Pentagon file clerk who misplaces a classified document faces stiffer penalties than a defense secretary whose arrogant recklessness consumes thousands of lives.

Failure does not yield apology or contrition or even acknowledgment of responsibility. Instead, it creates opportunities for yet more obfuscating explanations; in short, the chance to write a self-exculpatory memoir. "Look, not everything went right," Secretary of State Condoleezza Rice explained in shrugging off Iraq. "This is a very difficult cir-

cumstance. There were some things that went right and
some things that went wrong. And you know what? We will
have a chance to look at that in history. And I will have a
chance to reflect on that when I have a chance to write my
book."[19]

Faced with a choice of acknowledging an uncomfortable
truth or finding some way to conceal, spin, or deny that
truth, those who preside over the institutions of the national
security state invariably choose the latter.

As with the constitutional deformities that have produced the imperial presidency, one might overlook these
sins if the agencies forming the backbone of the national security state could point to a solid record of achievement. Yet
the reverse is true. Over the course of their existence, these
entities have done far more harm than good.

To make this case, the prosecution can call as its chief
witness the president of the United States. No one has been
more attuned to the defects of the national security state
than the client for whom it was created. Here is a great
irony: Over the last several decades, presidents have come
to view the national security apparatus not as an aid but as
an impediment in decision making. More often than not,
presidents come into office wary of any advice that these institutions might have on offer, suspecting that it is anything
but disinterested. Those not already educated in the ways of
Washington quickly learn that institutions nominally subordinate to executive authority pursue their own agendas and
will privilege their own purposes over those of whoever
happens to occupy the White House.

Dwight D. Eisenhower, a man who appreciated sound
staff work, was the last president to work through and with
the national security bureaucracy. During his eight years in
office, the National Security Council formally convened on

366 occasions, with meetings usually chaired by Ike himself.[20] The NSC system produced countless memoranda, studies, and directives, all of them carefully coordinated among the various national security agencies. Yet, although Eisenhower's highly structured approach to policy formulation maintained at least a modicum of discipline, the most important agencies eluded his control. The military services actively sought to undermine Eisenhower's policies or to distort them in pursuit of parochial interests.[21] The CIA functioned as a sovereign state within a state.[22]

As soon as he entered office in January 1961, John F. Kennedy jettisoned his predecessor's deliberate approach, which was at odds with Kennedy's own temperament and with the image that his administration wished to project. "New Frontiersmen" cultivated a style that placed a premium on informality, flexibility, and quickness. Kennedy and those around him believed that small groups of really bright people—people like themselves—could reach better decisions faster, if not encumbered by bureaucratic process. Fancying themselves as not only smart but also creative, they had little patience for the orthodoxies and conventions to which the national security apparatus professed devotion.

If Kennedy nursed any lingering thoughts of that apparatus proving itself useful, they did not survive the debacle of the Bay of Pigs. When JFK became president, plans to overthrow Cuba's Fidel Castro using a small force of CIA-trained and -equipped Cuban exiles were well advanced. Kennedy just needed to give the signal to launch the invasion. The new president hesitated, however, directing General Lyman Lemnitzer, chairman of the Joint Chiefs of Staff, to evaluate the plan's feasibility. When the Chiefs endorsed the operation, Kennedy issued the order. An epic disaster ensued.

It soon became apparent that the Chiefs had supported the mission less because they expected it to succeed than because they were counting on a CIA failure to pave the way for a conventional invasion, their preferred option for eliminating Castro. The Chiefs knew that Kennedy had no intention of ordering direct U.S. intervention—he had said as much—but they were counting on a presidentially ordered CIA disaster to force his hand. Rather than offering the president forthright professional advice, they had diddled him.

In the history of the national security state, the Bay of Pigs proved a turning point. A furious Kennedy, convinced (not without reason) that he had been set up and betrayed, drew two large conclusions from this experience.

First, the Bay of Pigs convinced him that the CIA's reputation for tackling tough jobs quietly and economically was wildly overinflated. The hapless invasion scheme hatched by the agency never had even a remote chance of inciting a successful counterrevolution. The intelligence on which it was based had been at best defective, at worst simply invented. The slapdash exile force assembled to invade Cuba lacked numbers, training, discipline, competent leadership, and essential equipment, as well as adequate air and logistics support. From planning to execution, the entire operation was amateurish and harebrained. All this was evident even within the agency—although, needless to say, the CIA classified its own scathing internal investigation of the affair, thereby concealing it from the public.[23]

Second, the Bay of Pigs convinced Kennedy that the Joint Chiefs of Staff, however many ribbons and medals they might have earned, were either stupid or untrustworthy.[24] "Those sons-of-bitches with all the fruit salad just sat there nodding, saying it would work," he grumbled.[25]

Whether the Chiefs were too dull or too clever by half, JFK concluded that allowing them any further say in the formulation of policy was a mistake. Although it might be necessary to go through the motions of consulting senior military leaders, never again would he defer to their collective judgment.

The education that Kennedy received as a result of his humiliation at the Bay of Pigs evoked a response that took three forms—worth recounting here because he was testing techniques similar to those his successors adopted to compensate for the inadequacies of the national security apparatus.

First, to prevent the CIA and the Chiefs from doing further damage, Kennedy moved decisively to change the leadership of each institution. He got rid of Lemnitzer and installed retired General Maxwell Taylor as chairman of the Joint Chiefs. In Taylor's view, it was incumbent upon any chairman to be "a true believer in the foreign policy and military strategy of the administration which he serves."[26] Taylor was just such a true believer—a Kennedy loyalist through and through. The president also replaced longtime CIA director Allen Dulles with John McCone. More ominously, behind the scenes, Kennedy directed his brother Robert, then attorney general, to take charge of the agency's most sensitive and highest priority mission: a now-redoubled effort to eliminate Fidel Castro. That the attorney general knew next to nothing about covert operations, sabotage, or assassination made no difference; his devotion to the president was beyond question—and that was the only credential he needed to oversee Operation Mongoose.

Having lost confidence in the CIA and the Joint Chiefs, Kennedy looked elsewhere for counsel, in effect creating alternative, presumably more competent centers of power.

This was the second response triggered by the Bay of Pigs. Henceforth, when the president sought advice, he turned increasingly to his special assistant for national security affairs, McGeorge Bundy, and to Secretary of Defense Robert McNamara. The governing assumption here was that Bundy (formerly dean of the Faculty of Arts and Sciences at Harvard), along with his deputy, W. W. Rostow (professor of economic history at MIT), and McNamara (formerly president of the Ford Motor Company), along with the Ph.D.-encrusted "Whiz Kids" he had hired to staff the Office of the Secretary of Defense, would offer the president more timely, concise, and cogent advice than he had gotten from connivers like Dulles and Lemnitzer. As Vietnam was to demonstrate, that governing assumption turned out to be false.

Kennedy's third response to the Bay of Pigs was to work around the national security apparatus altogether, extemporizing ad hoc entities that had no formal or statutory existence, but that he could institute or abolish as it suited him. The classic example that seemingly demonstrated the efficacy of this approach was the Ex Comm, improvised to advise Kennedy during the Cuban Missile Crisis. Throughout the famous Thirteen Days, the president never convened a formal meeting of the National Security Council and had but a single perfunctory interview with the Joint Chiefs, whose bellicose advice he politely ignored.

Once the crisis passed, the Ex Comm dissolved. Yet the idea of relying on such an entity—extraconstitutional, extralegal, deliberating in secret—retained enduring appeal. Though never officially reconstituted, the Ex Comm reappeared in many guises. Kennedy's successors regularly huddled with small groups of handpicked advisers, accountable to no one but the president himself, to consider which cities to attack, which countries to invade, which governments to subvert. Richard Nixon relied on an Ex Comm of two, consisting of himself and Henry Kissinger. When it came to serious matters—negotiating with the North Vietnamese or opening relations with China—consulting State or Defense was just about the last thing that either man cared to do. Yet the ultimate expression of Kennedy-style informality may have occurred during the administration of George W. Bush. The decision to invade Iraq seems to have emerged from a virtual Ex Comm, never constituted in the real world but reaching a consensus of sorts that provided the basis for action. The president never actually rendered a formal decision as such; his closest deputies proceeded as if he had.[27]

Meanwhile, the manifest failures of the CIA and the Chiefs, evident in episodes like the Bay of Pigs, inspired a cascade of proposals intended to "fix" these institutions. Indeed, efforts by reformers intent on correcting the deficiencies of the national security apparatus began well before Kennedy became president and continued long after his death. For good government types, figuring out how to make the CIA, the Pentagon, or the Joint Chiefs work has inspired countless study groups, blue-ribbon commissions, and congressional investigations. Proposals for institutional reform and reorganization began appearing almost as soon as the legislation creating the national security state was signed into law back in 1947, and these have remained hardy perennials ever since.[28] The push for such reforms after 9/11, for instance, produced yet another blue-ribbon commission that issued yet another glossy report that, in turn, inspired Congress to create a director of national intelligence assisted by a new Office of the Director of National Intelligence—all of which added an additional layer of bureaucracy to the sprawling U.S. Intelligence Community.

Yet to a considerable extent, this never-ending campaign—

with results always falling well short of predictions—
conceals the real story of the national security state, namely,
that, ever since Kennedy, presidents themselves and their
chief lieutenants have viewed the apparatus as irredeemably
broken. Former secretary of defense James Schlesinger's assessment of the Joint Chiefs of Staff applies to the national
security bureaucracy as a whole: Its advice "is generally ir-
relevant, normally unread, and almost always disregarded."[29]

For those who occupy the inner circle of power, the national security state is an obstacle to be evaded rather than
an asset to be harnessed. Viewed from the perspective of a
defense secretary or national security adviser, professional
military officers, career diplomats, or intelligence analysts
are not partners but competitors. Rather than facilitating the
exercise of executive power, the career professionals compli-
cate or even obstruct it, pursuing the favored agendas of their
own agencies instead. Yet because the institutions compris-
ing the national security apparatus provide the foundation
of executive power, the president-emperor is the person
least inclined to acknowledge publicly the defects inherent
in that apparatus. As a consequence, the American people
remain in the dark, persisting in the illusion that, whatever
their faults, institutions like the Joint Chiefs and the CIA remain indispensable to the nation's safety and well-being.

And so the national security state perdures. It does so
not because its activities enhance the security of the American people, but because, by its very existence, it provides a
continuing rationale for political arrangements that are a
source of status, influence, and considerable wealth. Lapses
in performance by this apparatus might logically raise
questions about whether or not the United States would be
better off without it. Instead, failures inspire new efforts to
reorganize and reform, which almost invariably translate

into further institutional expansion. The more the national security state screws up, the more sprawling it becomes. In the meantime, presidents occupy themselves cultivating ways to work around, ignore, or subvert those institutions.

The administration of George W. Bush came into office already seeing the national security state as the enemy. One day prior to the attacks of 9/11, Donald Rumsfeld gathered employees of the Defense Department into a Pentagon auditorium and made the point explicitly. "The topic today," the secretary of defense began,

> is an adversary that poses a threat, a serious threat, to the security of the United States of America. This adversary is one of the world's last bastions of central planning. It governs by dictating five-year plans. From a single capital, it attempts to impose its demands across time zones, continents, oceans and beyond. With brutal consistency, it stifles free thought and crushes new ideas. It disrupts the defense of the United States and places the lives of men and women in uniform at risk.
>
> Perhaps this adversary sounds like the former Soviet Union, but that enemy is gone: our foes are more subtle and implacable today. You may think I'm describing one of the last decrepit dictators of the world. But their day, too, is almost past, and they cannot match the strength and size of this adversary.
>
> The adversary's closer to home. It's the Pentagon bureaucracy.

Dealing with this enemy within so preoccupied Rumsfeld that he was all but oblivious to the actual adversaries who, even as he spoke, were less than twenty-four hours from launching a direct assault on his own headquarters.

Since September 11, 2001, the administration has continued to view that bureaucracy as hostile. Nominally, the national security state that failed to anticipate or deflect the
9/11 attacks has undergone yet another great shake-up. The
chief result has been to gather various agencies charged
with internal security—the Coast Guard, Secret Service, Federal Emergency Management Administration, and various
entities charged with immigration, customs, transportation
security, and border patrol—into yet another cabinet-level
department and to centralize and expand further the activities of the various agencies charged with intelligence collec-
tion and analysis. In essence, reform has added to an already
top-heavy executive branch two new bureaucracies: the Department of Homeland Security and the U.S. Intelligence
Community.

Meanwhile, President Bush, like President Kennedy and
his various successors, exerted himself to keep the national
security apparatus from getting in the way. He did this by
employing techniques that by now qualified as tried-and-
true: marginalizing components of the national security machinery deemed potentially troublesome; installing loyalists
in senior positions without regard to their actual qualifications; and, when convenient or necessary, circumventing the
structure altogether.

Even before 9/11, the Bush administration had sought to
marginalize the Joint Chiefs of Staff. It did so by succes-
sively appointing pliant mediocrities to the office of chairman, Generals Richard Myers and Peter Pace making
Maxwell Taylor look like a model of strong-willed independence. Back in the 1980s, reformers had sought to fix the
problems then seen as afflicting the Joint Chiefs by investing greater authority in the chairman at the expense of the
individual service chiefs. In the early 1990s, with General

Colin Powell presiding over the Joint Chiefs, President Bill
Clinton had learned the hard way that a savvy, charismatic
chairman with a mind of his own could make life miserable
for a commander in chief. In early 1993, Powell used the
gays-in-the-military controversy to royally embarrass the
new president and establish the terms of civil-military relations in the Clinton era. Later that year, Powell and his fellow
generals deftly ensured that blame for the Mogadishu fiasco, when eighteen American soldiers were killed in a bungled raid, landed squarely in the laps of civilian officials.

When Powell retired in 1993, Clinton chose as his replacement an un-Powell—someone lacking the moxie to im-
pede presidential freedom of action. President George W.
Bush (or more likely Secretary of Defense Donald Rumsfeld
acting on his behalf) continued this practice. In fact, Rumsfeld went a step further. Retribution for the indignities that
Clinton had suffered in 1993 at the hands of the Joint Chiefs
came exactly ten years later when Rumsfeld and his deputy,
Paul Wolfowitz, singled out for ritual humiliation the one
senior military officer who dared to express skepticism
about the forthcoming invasion of Iraq. In testimony before
the Senate Armed Services Committee in February 2003,
General Eric Shinseki, the army chief of staff, expressed the
view that occupying Iraq might pose a daunting challenge
and could require several hundred thousand troops. This
departed from the Bush administration's vague but rosy
predictions about the war and its aftermath. Shinseki's candor elicited immediate rebukes from Rumsfeld and his
deputy. The general's estimate was "wildly off the mark," an
obviously annoyed Wolfowitz informed the press. Shinseki
became persona non grata and was soon ushered into retirement.

Shinseki's fate offered an object lesson to his peers. In

Rumsfeld's Pentagon, generals did not ask questions; they did not express independent views, even to Congress; they did as they were told. No one got the word quicker than General Tommy Franks, the officer who as commander of U.S. Central Command planned and implemented the invasions of Afghanistan and Iraq. When it came to pleasing Rumsfeld, Franks was nothing if not eager. Asked by President Bush prior to the Iraq War to offer his own views, the general replied, "Sir, I think exactly what my secretary thinks, what he's ever thought, whatever he will ever think, or whatever he thought he might think."[30]

Senior officers themselves had contributed mightily to the atmosphere of civil-military mistrust that pervaded Washington as the United States embarked upon its global war on terror. Rumsfeld's heavy-handedness was, in a sense, civilian payback for double-dealing and game playing that could be traced back to the late 1940s, when obstreperous service chiefs essentially drove James Forrestal, the first secretary of defense, to an emotional breakdown and subsequent suicide. But if the Chiefs were getting what they deserved, the country as a whole paid a heavy price. Civilians like Rumsfeld no longer believed senior military leaders capable of offering professional military advice untainted by extraneous considerations. So, with Tommy Franks as the Bush administration's compliant enabler, the country proceeded to impale itself on Iraq.

A similar story applies to the Central Intelligence Agency. Although President Bush did not appoint George Tenet to his post—the CIA director was a hand-me-down from the Clinton era—he kept Tenet on, even after the agency's infamous intelligence failures of 9/11. The reason seems clear: The president could count on the eager-to-please Tenet to tell him what he wanted to hear. Famously, of course, Tenet assured the president that proving the existence of Iraqi weapons of mass destruction would be a "slam dunk," providing the essential rationale for a preventive war that Bush wished to launch for other reasons. Analysts within the State Department might have harbored doubts about the existence of Iraqi weapons of mass destruction (or about the wisdom of invading Iraq), but their views counted for little so long as Tenet was there to recite his lines.

Yet even with the subservient Tenet as CIA director, Secretary of Defense Rumsfeld worried about the agency obstructing administration plans to invade Iraq. In September 2002, he established within his own staff the Office of Special Plans (OSP) and assigned it the task of independently assessing intelligence related to Saddam Hussein's WMD program and his regime's alleged ties to Al Qaeda. The inspiration for this initiative was self-evident: Rumsfeld feared that, even with Tenet at the helm, the CIA's own analysts weren't going to follow their assigned script. Senior officials in OSD, within the staff of the National Security Council, and in the office of the vice president all subscribed to the view that the CIA was simply not to be trusted.

The creation of OSP touched off fierce controversy. Critics charged that the secretary of defense had staffed it with hawkish neoconservatives hankering for war and willing to cook the books if necessary to get it. Yet assume the best intentions on the part of those involved, and it remains a remarkable as well as deeply troubling episode: In effect, the Office of the Secretary of Defense was essentially charging the nation's premier intelligence agency with itself cooking the books on a security issue of paramount importance. Although the press tended to portray the issue as an illustration of the way Washington works—just a workaday example of interagency squabbling—it actually signified something far more telling: the collapse of the assumption that major national security agencies actually adhere to a common definition of the national interest.

The operative question becomes this: If neither the CIA nor the Joint Chiefs of Staff had existed when Osama bin Laden launched his attack, if Congress had not created the Department of Defense or the National Security Council back in 1947, would the United States find itself in any worse shape than it is? That is, if President Bush had had to rely upon the institutions that existed through World War II—a modest State Department for diplomacy and two small cabinet agencies to manage military affairs—would he have bollixed up Iraq any more than he already has? To frame the question more broadly: When considering the national security state as it has evolved and grown over the past six decades, what exactly has been the value added? And if the answer is none—if, indeed, the return on investment has been essentially negative—then perhaps the time has come to consider dismantling an apparatus that demonstrably serves no useful purpose.

Wise Men Without Wisdom

Given the manifest deficiencies of the national security apparatus, imperial presidents have looked elsewhere for counsel on matters of war and peace. To the extent that agencies such as the CIA or the Joint Chiefs of Staff tell presidents what they want to hear, their efforts might still retain some marginal utility. When it comes to making the tough calls, however, presidents have relied increasingly on a small circle of presumably trusty advisers rather than on a leaky, obstreperous bureaucracy. Personal loyalty to the president, not one's ranking on some organizational chart, has become the ultimate determinant of influence.

In the age of permanent national security crisis, serious issues are invariably taken up off-stage and behind closed doors. Here is where the real business of contemporary politics occurs. Here, the real action involves only a handful of players, for the most part unelected, their deliberations for the most part occurring behind a veil of secrecy.

From the outset, two fundamental convictions have informed this practice. The first is the belief that by consulting a cadre of handpicked Wise Men, presidents are likely to make better decisions. Although "the decider" may make the final call, the actual process of arriving at decisions proceeds collectively, with the president drawing on the counsel of smart, sophisticated, and worldly-wise advisers, who themselves tap the expertise of functionaries possessing more specialized knowledge.

The second conviction relates to the necessity of these advisers working exclusively for the chief executive and no one else. Only if assured that their counsel will remain shielded from the public will Wise Men speak with candor and honesty—here lies the basis for claims of "executive privilege."

Indeed, as a general proposition, Wise Men view popular—or even congressional—intrusion into policy formulation as distinctly unhelpful, if not downright dangerous. The intricacies of national security are said to lie beyond the ken of the average citizen, who is all too likely to be swayed by short-term, emotional considerations rather than taking a sober, long-term view. The masses, being notoriously fickle, are incapable of grasping such matters. They can't see the big picture. They don't appreciate nuance. They lack resolve. A president seeking a genuinely strategic approach will rely on seasoned insiders—rational, dispassionate, well-informed, well-connected, and guided by a common vocabulary and a common understanding of the way the world actually works.

By and large, members of the national security elite hold the public in remarkably low regard, although they typically keep that view under wraps. When speaking to the press, they pay homage to all of the familiar political clichés, alluding frequently and respectfully, for example, to "the will" of the American people.

From time to time, however, the mask slips and it becomes apparent that those on the inside don't care a fig for what members of the great unwashed might think. "If you truly had a democracy and did what the people wanted," Secretary of State Dean Acheson once remarked in passing, "you'd go wrong every time."[31] In addition to expressing his own personal view, Acheson's statement neatly summarizes one of the fundamental assumptions on which the national security elite bases its claim of authority: Public opinion is suspect; when it comes to national security, the public's anointed role is to defer. This means taking their cues from the likes of Dean Acheson, who himself explained how senior officials manufacture deference: by relying on propaganda. As he wrote in his memoirs, when offering public explanations of policy, "qualification must give way to simplicity, nicety and nuance to bluntness, almost brutality, to carry the point home." The idea is not to describe truth in all of its messy complexity, but to convey a point of view that is "clearer than truth."[32]

This presidential reliance on Wise Men is by no means a recent phenomenon. We can trace its origins at least as far back as Woodrow Wilson, who famously employed Colonel Edward M. House as his confidant, alter ego, and diplomatic troubleshooter. The heyday of the tradition occurred during World War II when a cadre of distinguished citizens rotated to Washington (more often than not from Wall Street) to occupy senior positions in the Roosevelt administration. Included in their ranks were Acheson, W. Averell Harriman, Robert Lovett, John J. McCloy, Robert Patterson, and above all Henry L. Stimson. This was the Eastern Establishment incarnate, its members accomplished, wealthy, and self-assured. Many had fought in World War I. All viewed government service in a time of national emergency as tantamount to duty. They were comfortable with power. They exuded confidence. They shared a worldview and a view of America's rightful place in the world.

It would be a mistake to romanticize this tradition, which in retrospect appears parochial, hidebound, and given to snobbery. Although its members evinced an admirable sense of noblesse oblige, they were largely oblivious to questions of social justice and human rights. On matters of race and religion, they reflected the prejudices characteristic of their class and their times. Yet there was no doubting their patriotism. Adherents to the Stimson tradition saw themselves as servants of the state. Although they were of conservative temperament, their labors transcended partisan considerations. Their aim was to preserve the United States rather than to tamper with the social or economic arrangements defining the American way of life. In the circumstances that existed in the 1940s, preserving the nation meant strengthening it—establishing beyond question America's place in the front rank of great powers. To a remarkable extent, Stimson and others like him succeeded in achieving their goal.

The end of World War II sounded the death knell of this tradition. We can date the beginning of its decline fairly precisely. It occurred on September 21, 1945, when Secretary of War Stimson, just turned seventy-eight, departed Washington for the last time, while Secretary of the Navy James Forrestal stayed on, becoming an increasingly influential figure.

The contrast between these two remarkable, if today largely forgotten, figures tells the story. Stimson was old-money Presbyterian, a graduate of Phillips Academy, Yale, and Harvard Law, and the epitome of the successful Wall Street lawyer. He married young and remained devoted to his wife. He accumulated a distinguished record of public service that included active duty in France in 1918, a stint as governor-general of the Philippines, four years as secretary of state, and two tours running the War Department. To his legions of admirers, Stimson represented "trust, truth, justice, virtue, the reign of law, the call of duty, [and] the shining example."[33]

Forrestal was Irish-Catholic, the son of impoverished immigrants. Although he attended Princeton, he dropped out before graduating. Gravitating to Wall Street, he joined the investment firm of Dillon, Read and demonstrated a gift for making money. Rising through the ranks, he became the firm's president in 1938. In 1940, he went to Washington and served in a succession of high positions. Forrestal's personal life was a shambles: His wife was a floozy and a drunk; he was himself a hard drinker, an inattentive father, and a compulsive womanizer. He was ambitious, erratic, insecure, combative, and resentful. Desperately lonely, Forrestal embraced government service in a vain effort to flee demons that had pursued him ever since boyhood.[34]

By the end of World War II, Secretary Stimson was the face of Old Washington. He had been around forever. He had seen it all. As such, he was not given to overreaction. He did

not panic. He represented steadiness, prudence, and so-
briety.

Forrestal signified an altogether different temperament,
combining a sense of alarm with a demand for immediate
action. He was a pseudorealist, purporting to see the world
as it was, yet badly misconstruing the situation actually facing the United States. Foreshadowing Dick Cheney's "One-
Percent Doctrine," Forrestal argued that to wait on events
was to incur unacceptable risk. Danger loomed just ahead
and demanded an urgent response. Even the slightest delay
invited apocalyptic defeat. Certainly, this was the spirit ani-
mating Forrestal's efforts beginning in 1945 to mobilize
Washington against the threat of what he called "Red fascism," a Stalinist regime hell-bent on applying the "principles of dialectical materialism everywhere" in order to
promote "world revolution."[35]

Forrestal did not possess large stores of wisdom. He
lacked balance, judgment, equanimity. He was, in fact, a
sick, tormented man. Yet he left a lasting mark on U.S. policy and an even greater mark on subsequent generations of
Wise Men. Professing to admire Stimson, they tended to
model themselves after Forrestal, sounding the alarm at the
drop of a hat. From the 1940s down to and including the
present decade, Forrestal's offspring found their way into
the inner circles of presidential advisers, nervously worry-
ing that the worst case just might be the most probable one
and urging prompt action to forestall disaster. The advo-
cates of the Iraq War number among his direct descendants.

Throughout his presidency, Dwight D. Eisenhower worried that a fearful America might one day become a "garrison state," a concern expressed most explicitly in his
Farewell Address. Although Eisenhower's warning remains
all too relevant—not least in emphasizing the need for "an

alert and knowledgeable citizenry" to guard against the abuse of power by a "military-industrial complex"—his worst fears have not materialized. The United States today is not a garrison state. Yet without question, American political elites have succumbed to a garrison mentality, obsessing about security and seeing military power as the optimum means to resolve international issues. James Forrestal is the godfather of that militarized mind-set.

If he had an immediate heir, it was Paul Nitze, a master at hyping the Threat and one of the most durable and influential of the postwar Wise Men. Like Forrestal, Nitze had made a fortune working for Dillon, Read during the interwar period. In 1940, he followed Forrestal to Washington and stayed on to become a fixture of the national security establishment. Across the next four decades, whether in government or hovering on the fringes, Nitze remained a major player in the politics of national security. Yet his most lasting contribution—signaling that the confrontational tradition of James Forrestal had superseded the more temperate tradition of Henry Stimson—came early on, when Nitze served as the principal author of NSC 68, a highly classified report drafted for President Truman and the National Security Council in early 1950.

Historians have long seen NSC 68 as one of the foundational documents of postwar American statecraft. From our present perspective, it is that and more. NSC 68 provides us with an early sense of what our postwar habit of deferring to Wise Men has wrought.

Two recent events had prompted Truman in January 1950 to direct the State and Defense departments to undertake an urgent—and of course secret—review of national security strategy. Although those events were by no means trivial, Nitze's chief contribution was to blow them completely out of proportion and use them as a basis to argue for a sweeping reorientation of U.S. policy. In this effort, he ultimately prevailed.

The first of those two events was the Soviet detonation of a nuclear device in August 1949. The Soviet test did not call into question overall U.S. nuclear superiority, nor did it even mean that the Kremlin yet possessed a deliverable weapon. Its immediate impact was largely psychological. The sudden disappearance of their absolute nuclear monopoly took Americans by surprise, ratcheting up the fear, already deeply embedded in the nation's collective subconscious, that cities like New York and San Francisco could one day suffer the fate of Hiroshima and Nagasaki.

The second event was the Chinese Revolution, which on October 1, 1949, established Communist Party leader Mao Zedong in a position of supreme authority over the Chinese mainland. In contrast to the Soviet nuclear test, this development did not come as a surprise. U.S. officials had for some time been expecting the Nationalists under Jiang Jieshi to lose their bitter struggle with the Communists. Yet even if the outcome was predictable, that did not make it welcome. From Washington's perspective, Beijing going Red constituted a major setback for the West. Even so, China under Mao remained a backward and impoverished nation incapable of threatening the United States. In Beijing, Communists had gained power, but that fact alone did not make of China a power.

Five years after the end of World War II, the United States stood at the very zenith of its own power and influence. Still, according to NSC 68, it now found itself in "deepest peril," with "the destruction not only of this Republic but of civilization itself" suddenly looming as a real possibility.[36] Indeed, the American system was "in greater jeopardy than ever before in our history." This, at least, was how Nitze described the situation facing the United States in the spring of 1950.

This sense of apocalyptic danger expressed Nitze's understanding of the Soviet Union and its intentions. "Animated by a new fanatic faith," the Kremlin was seeking "to impose its absolute authority over the rest of the world." The Soviet Union sought "to bring the free world under its dominion," relying on "infiltration and intimidation" backed up by "overwhelming military force." Toward that end, according to NSC 68, the Soviet program aimed at "the complete subversion and forcible destruction of the machinery of government and structure of society in the countries of the non-Soviet world and their replacement by an apparatus and structure subservient to and controlled by the Kremlin." "Persistent crisis, conflict, and expansion" defined the essence of Soviet policy. All of this stood in sharp contrast to America's benign posture, which expressed "the essential tolerance of our world outlook, our generous and constructive impulses, and the absence of covetousness in our international relations."

The contest joined in the aftermath of World War II pitted liberty against abject and all-encompassing slavery. Affirming that "the idea of freedom is the most contagious idea in history," NSC 68 went on to explain that the Soviets regarded freedom's mere existence as a "permanent and continuous threat." To destroy that threat, the Soviet leadership had launched a worldwide assault on free institutions. The Red Army offered proof of the Kremlin's nefarious intentions. NSC 68 professed alarm that "the Soviet Union actually possesses armed forces far in excess of those necessary to defend its national territory." According to Nitze's analysis, the Soviet Union—actually a country leveled by

World War II and barely in the recovery phase—already enjoyed a clear preponderance of power. Even so, day by day, it was "widening the gap between its preparedness for war and the unpreparedness of the free world for war."

To respond to this unprecedented threat, Nitze could divine only three options: isolationism; preventive war (which implied a nuclear first strike against a country incapable of responding in kind); or simply "a more rapid build-up" of American power, especially military power. NSC 68 rejected the first option as tantamount to capitulation. It dismissed the second as "repugnant" and "morally corrosive." That left only option number three. Nitze's proposed buildup called for massively increased defense spending, with particular emphasis on accelerating the development of a hydrogen bomb; increased security assistance to train and equip the armies of friendly nations; efforts to enhance internal security and intelligence capabilities; and an intensification of covert operations aimed at "fomenting and supporting unrest and revolt" inside the Soviet bloc. National security had to rank first among the nation's priorities, so NSC 68 called for curbing domestic expenditures. It also argued for higher taxes to make available the resources needed to fund rearmament. In effect, this "Nitze Doctrine" offered a recipe for the permanent militarization of U.S. policy.

Increased military spending need not imply belt-tightening by the average American, however. NSC 68 held out the prospect that "the economic effects of the program might be to increase the gross national product by more than the amount being absorbed for additional military and foreign assistance purposes." The United States, in other words, could afford both guns and butter—indeed, producing more guns might actually yield more butter.

For Nitze, this was a key selling point. Rather than being

at odds with the nation's long-term economic well-being, high levels of military spending could actually provide the basis for continuing prosperity—an argument clearly designed to win over members of the administration, especially President Truman himself, worried about the domestic implications of pouring huge sums of money into defense. Here lay one source of the Nitze Doctrine's enduring appeal: Rearmament promised not only greater security but also ever-greater material abundance.

Yet Truman remained unconvinced, until fate intervened in the form of the Korean War. For an increasingly beleaguered president, the outbreak of war on the Korean peninsula came as yet another unwelcome surprise. For Nitze, it was a timely bit of good luck. Communist North Korea's invasion of the south seemingly affirmed the analysis contained in NSC 68: International communism, responding to directives issued by the Kremlin, was apparently on the march. Not for the last time in recent American history—the Soviet invasion of Afghanistan in 1979 offers another example—Wise Men impulsively attributed earth-shattering significance to a development of middling importance. The result was to sweep aside remaining doubts about Nitze's prescription. NSC 68 became dogma. The defense budget more than tripled in size, most of the increased spending used not to fight in Korea but to fund the program of general rearmament that Nitze had proposed. The militarization of U.S. policy began in earnest.

Were this document merely an artifact of historical interest, it would not merit our attention here. But NSC 68 was much more than that. Although most Americans today are unfamiliar with its contents, Nitze's masterwork stands in relation to contemporary U.S. policy as Washington's Farewell Address or the Monroe Doctrine stood in relation to U.S. policy in the nineteenth century. It provides the interpretive key that explains much that was to follow over subsequent decades.

Even today, for neoconservatives like Max Boot, Thomas Donnelly, and Frederick Kagan, NSC 68 retains a talismanic significance, a model for what a "coherent grand strategy" ought to look like.[37] According to Kagan, a fellow at the American Enterprise Institute, Nitze's handiwork offers "a vision of the security policy America must pursue for as long as it is a global power."[38] Yet what some see as coherence appears in another light as extreme agitation laced with paranoia, delusions of grandeur, and a cavalier disregard for empirical truth. To read NSC 68 today is to enter a hothouse of apprehension, dread, and panic—the same combination of emotions that helped facilitate the Iraq War and with just as little connection to reality. NSC 68 was an exercise in fearmongering, which has remained the stock-in-trade of Wise Men from Nitze's day to the present.

The pattern has become a familiar one: Nitze-like figures with the status of Washington insiders cry havoc and clamor for immediate remedial action. Sometimes, as with the drafting of NSC 68, the ensuing sequence of events plays itself out behind closed doors. Just as often, it takes the form of a full-blown Washington-style melodrama. Congressional investigations are launched. Commissions convene. Think tanks issue thick reports that reinforce the growing sense of alarm. Leaks to the press create the impression that things may well be even worse than they seem. Always danger looms. ("Keep elevating the threat," Secretary of Defense Donald Rumsfeld urged his subordinates after 9/11. "Make the American people realize they are surrounded in the world by violent extremists.")[39] Always the United States is falling behind, and always the remedy lies in developing urgently needed new capabilities or underwriting greater activism—and, of course, pouring more money into the Pentagon, the intelligence services, and the rest of the national security apparatus.

In the years since its promulgation, the Nitze Doctrine has become a model to which members of the national security elite have repeatedly turned. Even today, the methods pioneered by Nitze in 1950 retain value. He demonstrated the advantages of demonizing America's adversaries, thereby transforming trivial concerns into serious threats and serious threats into existential ones. He devised the technique of artfully designing "options" to yield precooked conclusions, thereby allowing the analyst to become the de facto decision maker. He showed how easily American ideals could be employed to camouflage American ambitions, with terms like *peace* and *freedom* becoming code words for expansionism.[40] Above all, however, Nitze demonstrated the inestimable value of sowing panic as a means of driving the policy-making process. When it came to removing obstacles and loosening purse strings, the Nitze Doctrine worked wonders.

In the mid-1950s, with Nitze himself leading the charge, there came reports of a dismaying "bomber gap," the Soviets said to be outstripping the United States in the production of strategic bombers. Soon thereafter, rumors of a "missile gap" made headlines, with the Soviets reportedly far ahead of the United States in long-range rocketry. The ubiquitous Nitze served as principal author of the Gaither Report that trumpeted this concern.

By the end of the decade, insiders worried anxiously that Soviet strategic advantages were becoming so great as to undermine the "delicate balance of terror." The U.S. ability to deter its adversary was eroding and might soon disappear.

In the mid-1970s, then CIA director George H. W. Bush convened a group of Wise Men, Nitze prominent among them,
to investigate this concern. This so-called Team B exercise
concluded that things were even worse than suspected: The
United States was now lagging so far behind that a Soviet
first strike loomed as a real possibility. Hardly had the Soviet menace disappeared than the "Commission to Assess
the Ballistic Missile Threat to the United States," chaired by
Donald Rumsfeld in 1998, was warning that the United
States was underestimating the dangers posed by the missile programs of such nations as Iran, Iraq, and North Korea.

None of these, beginning with NSC 68's phantasmagoric
description of Soviet capabilities and intentions in 1950,
turned out to be accurate. In each and every case, proponents of the Nitze Doctrine garbled the facts and magnified
the danger. The bomber and missile gaps of the Eisenhower
era were figments of overactive imaginations. Even as its nuclear arsenal grew in the 1960s and 1970s, the Soviet Union
never achieved anything remotely like a preemptive capability. As for the Rumsfeld Commission, its conclusions have
proven entirely bogus. Yet in each of these cases, as with
NSC 68, the hue and cry concocted by Wise Men produced
the intended result.

In each case, as with NSC 68 itself, purportedly rigorous
analysis actually served to disguise an exercise in group-
think, yielding preconceived conclusions that reflected the
prejudices, policy agendas, and career interests of the prin-
cipals involved. George W. Bush's lieutenants did not invent
the idea of "fixing" the facts to fit a particular policy.[41] They
merely elevated to new heights of audacity a technique that
has played a central role in the politics of national security
over the past sixty years.

In our own day, the prince of audacity has been Paul

Wolfowitz. Just as Nitze was Forrestal's heir, so Wolfowitz deserves to be seen as Nitze's offspring. During the 1970s, Wolfowitz first made his mark serving with Nitze as a junior member of Team B. During the 1990s, he resurfaced as a senior member of the Rumsfeld Commission. In between, he held various positions in the State and Defense departments, steadily advancing up the organizational ladder. Although little known to the public, among insiders Wolfowitz acquired a reputation as a rising star—cerebral, imaginative, acutely sensitive to new perils lurking just over the horizon, and impatient with the inhibitions imposed by received wisdom.

For Wolfowitz, the ideology of national security served as a sort of surrogate religion. He was a true believer, harboring no doubts about history's purpose and America's assigned role in accomplishing that purpose. Viewing American power as bountiful and self-replenishing, Wolfowitz had always been keen to put that power to work. If anything, the end of the Cold War only accentuated this activist inclination. Wolfowitz shared in the view that victory had vaulted the United States to a position of overwhelming preeminence. "With so great a capacity to influence events," he wrote, "comes a requirement to figure out how best to use that capacity to shape the future."[42] Besides, the risks of inaction, although difficult to gauge, were in his judgment likely to outweigh the risks of action.

In his own approach to shaping the future, Wolfowitz assigned a central role to military power. While serving in the Defense Department under the elder President Bush, he achieved brief notoriety as the reputed author of a document making the case for permanent and unquestioned global military supremacy as the cornerstone of post–Cold War policy. Critics, mostly Democrats, derided the proposal as a blueprint for a militarized Pax Americana. When a Democrat gained the White House in 1993, however, he proceeded to foster a Pax Americana–lite, generously seasoned with American military might. As Bill Clinton dispatched U.S. troops to Somalia, Haiti, and the Balkans, as U.S. missiles and bombs blasted Serbs, Sudanese, Afghans, and Iraqis, Wolfowitz's complaint was not that U.S. policy had become too reckless but that it remained too timid. He chided "the Clinton administration's tendency to temporize rather than go for the jugular." This temporizing "had the effect of piling up future problems."[43] Wolfowitz wasn't interested in piling up problems; he wanted to raze them.

The events of September 11, 2001, found Wolfowitz once more in government, now the second-ranking official in George W. Bush's Department of Defense. For Wolfowitz, the murder of nearly three thousand Americans was a terrible tragedy that opened up a rich vein of opportunity. Here was the chance to end once and for all any further tendency to temporize. Just as Nitze had seized upon the Soviet bomb, the Chinese Revolution, and later the Korean War to argue for rebuilding American military power, so Wolfowitz now seized upon the attack by Al Qaeda to argue for unleashing American military might. As he saw it, the moment to go for the jugular had manifestly arrived.

Iraq offered the means to that end. The alleged threat posed by Iraqi weapons of mass destruction lent urgency to administration calls for action—the prospect of Saddam Hussein putting such weapons in the hands of terrorists becoming, as Wolfowitz later commented, "the one issue everyone could agree on."[44] The suffering of the Iraqi people under the boot of Saddam Hussein imbued the prospective conflict with a convenient moral pretext, allowing the administration to style a war of choice as a war of liberation.

Wolfowitz expected such a war to be transformative. Deposing Saddam would become the "moment in history when the West defined itself for the 21st Century"—that definition centered, of course, on "the values of freedom and democracy."[45] Toppling Saddam just might trigger a wave of political change across the Islamic world. Wolfowitz himself counted on "the liberation of the talented people of one of the most important Arab countries in the world" to create "an opportunity for Americans and Arabs and other people of good will" henceforth to live in peace and harmony. He found it "hard to believe" that any other outcome could result.[46]

Yet all of this amounted to garnish. For Wolfowitz, the main purpose of the Iraq War was to establish new norms governing the use of force. Nominally, the object of the exercise might be to eliminate weapons of mass destruction, overthrow a brutal dictator, and begin draining the terrorist "swamp." More fundamentally, the objective was to lift any and all restrictions on the use of armed force by the United States.

So the aftermath of 9/11 found Wolfowitz venturing into precincts where Nitze himself had feared to tread, advocating a policy of "anticipatory self-defense," a euphemism for preventive war. Within forty-eight hours of the attack on the World Trade Center and the Pentagon, he was already declaring categorically that, in its response to 9/11, the United States had no intention of confining its actions to those directly involved in the terrorist conspiracy. Bringing Osama bin Laden and his associates to justice would not suffice. Rather, the United States was intent on undertaking "a broad and sustained campaign" against any and all states posing a potential threat. The aim went beyond targeting would-be terrorists themselves. The United States meant to

deprive terrorists of sanctuaries or "safe havens" by nothing
less than a policy of "ending states who support terrorism."
In NSC 68, Nitze had at least made a pretense of offering
several options for consideration. For Wolfowitz after 9/11,
there existed only a single option: open-ended global war.

Within hours of the 9/11 attacks, Wolfowitz was already
pressing for military action to eliminate Saddam Hussein.
As a result, critics subsequently tagged him with being a
key architect of the Iraq War. A far more serious charge finds
him primarily responsible for legitimating the concept of
preventive war. History will remember Paul Wolfowitz as
the intellectual Svengali who conjured up the Bush Doctrine. In NSC 68, Nitze had rejected preventive war as "repugnant." Wolfowitz now promoted it as permissible,
essential, even inviting.

To most Americans prior to 1940, the idea of seeking permanent global military ascendancy seemed vaguely alien. It
was the sort of prospect that might have excited Prussians
but was unlikely to play well in Peoria. After 1950, the notion that the United States might content itself with anything less than a position of unquestioned military primacy
had become intolerable. This was the measure of what Nitze
had achieved.

Yet prior to 2001, despite the garrison mentality that
Nitze had done so much to promote, most Americans still
professed to see force as a last resort. Politicians still regarded war as something to be avoided, if at all possible. As
for preventive war, it lay beyond the pale. After 9/11, preventive war was enshrined as a core principle of U.S. policy.
Politicians of various stripes declared their support for
"global war," their enthusiasm undimmed by predictions
that the conflict was likely to continue for decades or even
generations. In effect, for the United States war had become

a permanent condition. Within Washington, at least, this re-markable development occurred without provoking the slightest interest in exploring the political, economic, social, or moral implications of a war without end. That any alter-native to global war might exist was a possibility that went unexamined. Here was the measure of what Wolfowitz had achieved during the months that culminated with the inva-sion of Iraq.

Niebuhr once wrote that the "false security to which all men are tempted is the security of power."[47] The Wise Men of the postwar era, from Forrestal through Nitze to Wol-fowitz, have never wavered in their devotion to this meretri-cious conception of security.

War Without End

The Bush Doctrine represents the most momentous national security initiative since the inauguration of the Manhattan Project that built the first atomic bomb. Its implications far outstrip in importance the eponymous doctrines of Presi-dents Truman, Eisenhower, Nixon, Carter, or Reagan.

Needless to say, in formulating this doctrine the Bush administration did not seek congressional assent. Nor did it even go through the motions of consulting the American people. A handful of Wise Men, led by Wolfowitz, saw a great opportunity to revolutionize national security policy. They wasted no time in exploiting that opportunity, selling the president on the merits of their idea and then imple-menting it, essentially by fiat.

The Bush Doctrine provided the ultimate rationale for invading Iraq. Wolfowitz and others in the administration were confident of achieving a quick, decisive victory. Indeed, the principal appeal of Iraq as a target was not that it was strong and fearsome; Gulf War I and a decade of sanctions had left Saddam Hussein with a decrepit army and essentially no air force. Iraq was inviting because it appeared so weak. An invasion promised to be a "cakewalk." Wolfowitz and others in the administration were counting on victory, in turn, to validate the Bush Doctrine, demonstrating its efficacy and thereby paving the way for its further application. Simply put, with victory in Iraq, any last constraints on the employment of U.S. military power (and on the prerogatives of the imperial presidency) would fall away.

It is important to appreciate the scope of the plans that 9/11 set in motion. Our fixation on all that has since gone wrong in Iraq itself should not lead us to overlook the fact that eliminating Saddam was never the endgame. The invasion of Iraq formed only one element of a breathtakingly extravagant design. The Wise Men to whom President Bush turned for advice after 9/11 expected an easy win against a weak opponent to set the stage for far greater victories.

As early as 1997, Wolfowitz had argued that with Saddam's removal "new options will open for U.S. policy." New options implied alluring new opportunities to wield American power, thereby shaping the future in accordance with American interests. "Actions that are difficult or impossible now," Wolfowitz had breezily predicted, "will become more feasible after we have taken the first steps."[48] Here lay the underlying intent of the Bush Doctrine: It provided a self-validating authorization for the administration to pursue whatever next steps it chose to take.

Although the next steps remained hidden from public view, they promised to be large. "We're an empire now, and when we act, we create our own reality," a senior Bush administration official famously remarked to the journalist

Ron Suskind. "We're history's actors . . . and you, all of you, will be left to just study what we do."[49] The Bush Doctrine offered the principal vehicle for creating that reality. Relying on military power, the White House would act. Everyone else—the bureaucracy, the Congress, the American people, and the rest of the world—would be left to watch.

As it turned out, of course, accomplishing those first steps proved to be far more difficult than Wolfowitz anticipated. Today, Iraq stands as the ultimate expression of what our habit of deference to Wise Men imbued with the ideology of national security has produced. The first application of the Bush Doctrine produced a shipwreck.

Efforts to identify the lessons to be learned from that catastrophe have focused on operational matters. The United States needs better intelligence, we are told. The armed forces must improve their counterinsurgency capabilities and do a better job of planning Phase IV—the panoply of activities entailed in occupying and rehabilitating a defeated country in the "next war." Soldiers need better equipment, whether to withstand attacks by Improvised Explosive Devices or to discriminate between insurgents and innocent civilians, killing the former while sparing the latter.

Yet this preoccupation with tactics and operations diverts attention from far more critical failings in the realm of politics. In that regard, the Iraq War—placed in the larger context of national security policy since 1945—should teach us the following.

First, the ideology of national security, American exceptionalism in its most baleful form, poses an insurmountable obstacle to sound policy. When American power was ascendant, the United States could pretend to interpret history's purpose or God's will. Today, it can no longer afford to indulge in such conceits.

Niebuhr once wrote that "the whole drama of history is enacted in a frame of meaning too large for human comprehension or management."[50] Acknowledging the truth of that dictum ought to be a prerequisite for election or appointment to high office. If policy makers persist in pretending otherwise, they will court disasters that may yet make the ongoing misadventure in Iraq appear almost trivial.

Second, Americans can no longer afford to underwrite a government that does not work. A condition of quasi-permanent crisis stretching across generations has distorted our Constitution with near-disastrous results. To imagine at this juncture that installing some fresh face in the White House, transferring the control of Congress from one party to the other, or embarking upon yet another effort to fix the national security apparatus will make much of a difference is to ignore decades of experience.

Yet if presidents have accrued too much power, if the Congress is feckless, if the national security bureaucracy is irretrievably broken, the American people have only themselves to blame. They have allowed their democracy to be hijacked. The hijackers will not voluntarily return what they have stolen.

One result of that hijacking has been to raise up a new political elite whose members have a vested interest in perpetuating the crises that provide the source of their power. These are the people who under the guise of seeking peace or advancing the cause of liberty devise policies that promote war or the prospect of war, producing something akin to chaos.

To attend any longer to this elite would be madness. This is the third lesson that the Iraq War ought to drive home. What today's Wise Men have on offer represents the inverse of wisdom. Indeed, to judge by the reckless misjudgments that have characterized U.S. policy since 9/11, presidents would be better served if they relied on the common sense of randomly chosen citizens rather than consulting sophisticated insiders. It is, after all, the children and grandchildren of ordinary citizens who end up fighting the wars that Wise Men concoct.

The Wise Men may not be overtly or consciously malevolent. To charge them with inventing threats out of whole cloth would be manifestly unfair. Yet from the era of Forrestal and Nitze to the present, they have repeatedly misconstrued and exaggerated existing threats, with perverse effects.

No doubt today's Wise Men see themselves as devoted patriots. No doubt they even mean well. Yet that's not good enough. As Paul Wolfowitz himself wrote, "No U.S. president can justify a policy that fails to achieve its intended results by pointing to the purity and rectitude of his intentions."[51] Much the same can be said of those who advise presidents and whose advice yields horrific consequences of the sort we have endured beginning on 9/11 and continuing ever since. They have forfeited any further claim to trust.

3. The Military Crisis

War is the great auditor of institutions," the historian Corelli Barnett once observed.[1] Since 9/11, the United States has undergone such an audit and been found wanting. That adverse judgment applies in full to America's armed forces.

Valor does not offer the measure of an army's greatness, nor does fortitude, nor durability, nor technological sophistication. A great army is one that accomplishes its assigned mission. Since George W. Bush inaugurated his global war on terror, the armed forces of the United States have failed to meet that standard.

In the aftermath of September 11, 2001, Bush conceived of a bold, offensive strategy, vowing to "take the battle to the enemy, disrupt his plans, and confront the worst threats before they emerge."[2] The military offered the principal means for undertaking this offensive, and U.S. forces soon found themselves engaged on several fronts.

Two of those fronts—Afghanistan and Iraq—commanded priority attention. In each case, the assigned task was to deliver a knockout blow, leading to a quick, decisive, economical, politically meaningful victory. In each case, despite impressive displays of valor, fortitude, durability, and technological sophistication, America's military came up short. The problem lay not with the level of exertion but with the results achieved.

In Afghanistan, U.S. forces failed to eliminate the leadership of Al Qaeda. Although they toppled the Taliban regime that had ruled most of that country, they failed to eliminate the Taliban movement, which soon began to claw its way back. Intended as a brief campaign, the Afghan War became a protracted one. Nearly seven years after it began, there is no end in sight. If anything, America's adversaries are gaining strength. The outcome remains much in doubt.

In Iraq, events followed a similar pattern, with the appearance of easy success belied by subsequent developments. The U.S. invasion began on March 19, 2003. Six weeks later, against the backdrop of a White House–produced banner proclaiming "Mission Accomplished," President Bush declared that "major combat operations in Iraq have ended." This claim proved illusory.

Writing shortly after the fall of Baghdad, the influential neoconservatives David Frum and Richard Perle declared Operation Iraqi Freedom "a vivid and compelling demonstration of America's ability to win swift and total victory."[3] General Tommy Franks, commanding the force that invaded Iraq, modestly characterized the results of his handiwork as "unequalled in its excellence by anything in the annals of war."[4] In retrospect, such judgments—and they were legion—can only be considered risible. A war thought to have ended on April 9, 2003, in Baghdad's al-Firdos

Square was only just beginning. Fighting dragged on for years, exacting a cruel toll. Iraq became a reprise of Vietnam, although in some respects at least on a blessedly smaller scale.

It wasn't supposed to be this way. Just a few short years ago, observers were proclaiming that the United States possessed military power such as the world had never seen. Here was the nation's strong suit. "The troops" appeared unbeatable. Writing in 2002, for example, Max Boot, a well-known commentator on military matters, attributed to the United States a level of martial excellence "that far surpasses the capabilities of such previous would-be hegemons as Rome, Britain, and Napoleonic France." With U.S. forces enjoying "unparalleled strength in every facet of warfare," allies, he wrote, had become an encumbrance: "We just don't need anyone else's help very much."[5]

Boot dubbed this the Doctrine of the Big Enchilada. Within a year, after U.S. troops had occupied Baghdad, he went further: America's army even outclassed Germany's *Wehrmacht*. The mastery displayed in knocking off Saddam, Boot gushed, made "fabled generals such as Erwin Rommel and Heinz Guderian seem positively incompetent by comparison."[6]

All of this turned out to be hot air. If the global war on terror has produced one undeniable conclusion, it is this: Estimates of U.S. military capabilities have turned out to be wildly overstated. The Bush administration's misplaced confidence in the efficacy of American arms represents a strategic misjudgment that has cost the country dearly. Even in an age of stealth, precision weapons, and instant communications, armed force is not a panacea. Even in a supposedly unipolar era, American military power turns out to be quite limited.

How did it happen that Americans so utterly overappraised the utility of military power? The answer to that question lies at the intersection of three great illusions.

According to the first illusion, the United States during the 1980s and 1990s had succeeded in reinventing armed conflict. The result was to make force more precise, more discriminating, and potentially more humane. The Pentagon had devised a new American Way of War, investing its forces with capabilities unlike any the world had ever seen. As President Bush exuberantly declared shortly after the fall of Baghdad in April 2003, "We've applied the new powers of technology . . . to strike an enemy force with speed and incredible precision. By a combination of creative strategies and advanced technologies, we are redefining war on our terms. In this new era of warfare, we can target a regime, not a nation."[7]

The distinction between regime and nation was a crucial one. By employing these new military techniques, the United States could eliminate an obstreperous foreign leader and his cronies, while sparing the population over which that leader ruled. Putting a missile through the roof of a presidential palace made it unnecessary to incinerate an entire capital city, endowing force with hitherto undreamed-of political utility and easing ancient moral inhibitions on the use of force. Force had been a club; it now became a scalpel. By the time the president spoke, such sentiments had already become commonplace among many (although by no means all) military officers and national security experts.

Here lay a formula for certain victory. Confidence in military prowess both reflected and reinforced a post–Cold War confidence in the universality of American values. Harnessed together, they made a seemingly unstoppable one-two punch.

With that combination came expanded ambitions. In the 1990s, the very purpose of the Department of Defense changed. Sustaining American global preeminence, rather than mere national security, became its explicit function. In the most comprehensive articulation of this new American Way of War, the Joint Chiefs of Staff committed the armed services to achieving what they called "full spectrum dominance"—unambiguous supremacy in all forms of warfare, to be achieved by tapping the potential of two "enablers"—"technological innovation and information superiority."[8]

Full spectrum dominance stood in relation to military affairs as the political scientist Francis Fukuyama's well-known proclamation of "the end of history" stood in relation to ideology: Each claimed to have unlocked ultimate truths. According to Fukuyama, democratic capitalism represented the final stage in political economic evolution. According to the proponents of full spectrum dominance, that concept represented the final stage in the evolution of modern warfare. In their first days and weeks, the successive invasions of Afghanistan and Iraq both seemed to affirm such claims.

According to the second illusion, American civilian and military leaders subscribed to a common set of principles for employing their now-dominant forces. Adherence to these principles promised to prevent any recurrence of the sort of disaster that had befallen the nation in Vietnam. If politicians went off half-cocked, as President Lyndon Johnson and Secretary of Defense Robert McNamara had back in the 1960s, generals who had correctly discerned and assimilated the lessons of modern war could be counted on to rein them in.

These principles found authoritative expression in the

Weinberger-Powell Doctrine, which specified criteria for deciding when and how to use force. Caspar Weinberger, secretary of defense during most of the Reagan era, first articulated these principles in 1984. General Colin Powell, chairman of the Joint Chiefs of Staff during the early 1990s, expanded on them. Yet the doctrine's real authors were the members of the post-Vietnam officer corps. The Weinberger-Powell principles expressed the military's own lessons taken from that war. Those principles also expressed the determination of senior officers to prevent any recurrence of Vietnam.

Henceforth, according to Weinberger and Powell, the United States would fight only when genuinely vital interests were at stake. It would do so in pursuit of concrete and attainable objectives. It would mobilize the necessary resources—political and moral as well as material—to win promptly and decisively. It would end conflicts expeditiously and then get out, leaving no loose ends. The spirit of the Weinberger-Powell Doctrine was not permissive; its purpose was to curb the reckless or imprudent inclinations of bellicose civilians.

According to the third illusion, the military and American society had successfully patched up the differences that produced something akin to divorce during the divisive Vietnam years. By the 1990s, a reconciliation of sorts was under way. In the wake of Operation Desert Storm, "the American people fell in love again with their armed forces." So, at least, General Colin Powell, one of that war's great heroes, believed.[9] Out of this love affair a new civil-military compact had evolved, one based on the confidence that, in times of duress, Americans could be counted on to "support the troops." Never again would the nation abandon its soldiers.

The All-Volunteer Force (AVF)—despite its name, a professional military establishment—represented the chief manifestation of this new compact. By the 1990s, Americans were celebrating the AVF as the one component of the federal government that actually worked as advertised. The AVF embodied the nation's claim to the status of sole superpower; it was "America's Team." In the wake of the Cold War, the AVF sustained the global Pax Americana without interfering with the average American's pursuit of life, liberty, and happiness. What was not to like?

Events since 9/11 have exposed these three illusions for what they were. When tested, the new American Way of War yielded more glitter than gold. The generals and admirals who touted the wonders of full spectrum dominance were guilty of flagrant professional malpractice, if not outright fraud. To judge by the record of the past twenty years, U.S. forces win decisively only when the enemy obligingly fights on American terms—and Saddam Hussein's demise has drastically reduced the likelihood of finding such accommodating adversaries in the future. As for loose ends, from Somalia to the Balkans, from Central Asia to the Persian Gulf, they have been endemic.

When it came to the Weinberger-Powell Doctrine, civilian willingness to conform to its provisions proved to be highly contingent. Confronting Powell in 1993, Madeleine Albright famously demanded to know, "What's the point of having this superb military that you're always talking about, if we can't use it?"[10] Mesmerized by the prospects of putting American soldiers to work to alleviate the world's ills, Albright soon enough got her way. An odd alliance that combined left-leaning do-gooders with jingoistic politicians and pundits succeeded in chipping away at constraints on the use of force. "Humanitarian intervention" became all the rage. Whatever restraining influence the generals exercised during the 1990s did not survive that decade. Lessons of Vietnam that had once seemed indelible were forgotten.

Meanwhile, the reconciliation of the people and the army turned out to be a chimera. When the chips were down, "supporting the troops" elicited plenty of posturing but little by way of binding commitments. Far from producing a stampede of eager recruits keen to don a uniform, the events of 9/11 reaffirmed a widespread popular preference for hiring someone else's kid to chase terrorists, spread democracy, and ensure access to the world's energy reserves. In the midst of a global war of ostensibly earthshaking importance, Americans demonstrated a greater affinity for their hometown sports heroes than for the soldiers defending the distant precincts of the American imperium. Tom Brady makes millions playing quarterback in the NFL and rakes in millions more from endorsements. Pat Tillman quit professional football to become an army ranger and was killed in Afghanistan. Yet, of the two, Brady more fully embodies the contemporary understanding of the term *Patriot*.

While they persisted, however, these three illusions fostered gaudy expectations about the efficacy of American military might. Every president since Ronald Reagan has endorsed these expectations. Every president since Reagan has exploited his role as commander in chief to expand on the imperial prerogatives of his office. Each has also relied on military power to conceal or manage problems that stemmed from the nation's habits of profligacy.

In the wake of 9/11, these puerile expectations—that armed force wielded by a strong-willed chief executive could do just about anything—reached an apotheosis of sorts. Having manifestly failed to anticipate or prevent a

devastating attack on American soil, President Bush proceeded to use his ensuing global war on terror as a pretext
for advancing grandiose new military ambitions married to
claims of unbounded executive authority—all under the
guise of keeping Americans "safe." With the president
denying any connection between the events of September 11
and past U.S. policies, his declaration of a global war nipped
in the bud whatever inclination the public might have entertained to reconsider those policies. In essence, Bush counted
on war both to concentrate greater power in his own hands
and to divert attention from the political, economic, and cultural bind in which the United States found itself as a result
of its own past behavior.

As long as U.S. forces sustained their reputation for in-
vincibility, it remained possible to pretend that the constitutional order and the American way of life were in good
health. The concept of waging an open-ended global campaign to eliminate terrorism retained a modicum of plausi-
bility. After all, how could anyone or anything stop the
unstoppable American soldier? Call that reputation into
question, however, and everything else unravels. This is
what occurred when the Iraq War went sour. The ills afflicting our political system, including a deeply irresponsible
Congress, broken national security institutions, and above
all an imperial commander in chief not up to the job, became all but impossible to ignore. So, too, did the self-
destructive elements inherent in the American way of
life—especially an increasingly costly addiction to foreign
oil, universally deplored and almost as universally indulged. More noteworthy still, the prospect of waging war
on a global scale for decades, if not generations, became pre-
posterous.

To anyone with eyes to see, the events of the past seven

years have demolished the Doctrine of the Big Enchilada. A gung-ho journalist like Robert Kaplan might still believe that, with the dawn of the twenty-first century, the Pentagon had "appropriated the entire earth, and was ready to flood the most obscure areas of it with troops at a moment's notice," that planet Earth in its entirety had become "battle space for the American military."[11] Yet any buck sergeant of even middling intelligence knew better than to buy such claptrap. With the Afghanistan War well into its seventh year and the Iraq War marking its fifth anniversary, a commentator like Michael Barone might express absolute certainty that "just about no mission is impossible for the United States military."[12] But Barone was not facing the prospect of being ordered back to the war zone for his second or third combat tour.

Between what President Bush called upon America's soldiers to do and what they were capable of doing loomed a huge gap that defines the military crisis besetting the United States today. For a nation accustomed to seeing military power as its trump card, the implications of that gap are monumental.

Learning the Wrong Lessons

To appreciate the full extent of this military crisis requires understanding what the Iraq War and, to a lesser extent, the Afghan War have to teach. These two conflicts, along with 9/11 itself, will form the centerpiece of George W. Bush's legacy. Their lessons ought to constitute the basis of a new, more realistic military policy.

In some respects, the effort to divine those lessons is well under way, spurred by critics of President Bush's policies on the left and the right as well as by reform-minded members of the officer corps. Broadly speaking, this effort has thus far yielded three distinct conclusions. Whether taken singly or together, they invert the post–Cold War military illusions that provided the foundation for the president's global war on terror. In exchange for these received illusions, they propound new ones, which are equally misguided. Thus far, that is, the lessons drawn from America's post-9/11 military experience are the wrong ones.

According to the first lesson, the armed services—and above all the army—need to recognize that the challenges posed by Iraq and Afghanistan define not only the military's present but also its future, the "next war," as enthusiasts like to say. Rooting out insurgents, nation-building, training and advising "host nation" forces, population security and control, winning hearts and minds—these promise to be ongoing priorities, preoccupying U.S. troops for decades to come, all across the Islamic world.

Rather than brief interventions ending in decisive victory, sustained presence will be the norm. Large-scale conventional conflict like 1991's Operation Desert Storm becomes the least likely contingency. The future will be one of small wars, expected to be frequent, protracted, perhaps perpetual.

Although advanced technology will retain an important place in such conflicts, it will not be decisive. Wherever possible, the warrior will rely on "nonkinetic" methods, functioning as diplomat, mediator, and relief worker.[13] No doubt American soldiers will engage in combat, but, drawing on the latest findings of social science, they will also demonstrate cultural sensitivity, not to speak of mastering local languages and customs. As Secretary of Defense Robert Gates put it in October 2007, "Reviving public services, rebuilding infrastructure and promoting good governance" had now become soldiers' business. "All these so-called nontraditional capabilities have moved into the mainstream of military thinking, planning, and strategy—where they must stay."[14]

This prospect implies a rigorous integration of military action with political purpose. Hard power and soft power will merge. The soldier on the ground will serve as both cop and social worker. This prospect also implies shedding the sort of utopian expectations that produced so much confident talk of "transformation," "shock-and-awe," and "network-centric warfare"—all of which had tended to segregate war and politics into separate compartments.

Local conditions will dictate technique, dooming the Pentagon's effort to devise a single preconceived, techno-logically determined template applicable across the entire spectrum of conflict. When it comes to low-intensity wars, the armed services will embrace a style owing less to the traditions of the Civil War, World War II, or even Gulf War I than to the nearly forgotten American experiences in the Philippines after 1898 and in Central America during the 1920s. Instead of looking for inspiration at the campaigns of U. S. Grant, George Patton, or H. Norman Schwarzkopf, of-ficers will study postwar British and French involvement in places like Palestine and Malaya, Indochina and Algeria.[15]

In sum, an officer corps bloodied in Iraq and Afghani-stan has seen the future and it points to many more Iraqs and Afghanistans. Whereas the architects of full spectrum dominance had expected the unprecedented lethality, range, accuracy, and responsiveness of high-tech striking power to perpetuate military dominion, the veterans of Iraq and Afghanistan know better. They remain committed to global dominance while believing that its pursuit will require not only advanced weaponry but also the ability to put boots on the ground and keep them there. This, in turn, implies a plentiful supply of soldiers and loads of patience on the home front.

Viewed from another perspective, however, the post-9/11 wars teach an altogether different lesson. According to this alternative view, echoing a similar complaint during the Vietnam era, the shortcomings of U.S. policy in Iraq and Afghanistan have little to do with the actual performance of American forces in the field and everything to do with the meddling of bumbling civilians back in Washington. In its simplest form, fault lies not with the troops themselves, nor with their commanders, but with the likes of Secretary of Defense Donald Rumsfeld, Deputy Secretary of Defense Paul Wolfowitz, and Undersecretary of Defense Douglas Feith, who prevented the troops from doing their jobs.

The charges leveled by Major General John Batiste, who served in Rumsfeld's Pentagon but subsequently retired in disgust and became one of the defense secretary's loudest military critics, are representative of this view. "Rumsfeld's dismal strategic decisions resulted in the unnecessary deaths of American servicemen and women," Batiste declared in September 2006. The former general held Rumsfeld personally "responsible for America and her allies going to war with the wrong plan." But that was just for starters. Rumsfeld also

> violated fundamental principles of war, dismissed deliberate military planning, ignored the hard work to build the peace after the fall of Saddam Hussein, set the conditions for Abu Ghraib and other atrocities that further ignited the insurgency, disbanded Iraqi security force institutions when we needed them

>most, [and] constrained our commanders with an
>overly restrictive de-Ba'athification policy.

Nor was the problem limited to Rumsfeld himself. It included his chief lieutenants. According to Batiste, Rumsfeld surrounded himself "with like-minded and compliant subordinates who [did] not grasp the importance of the principles of war, the complexities of Iraq, or the human dimension of warfare." The overall effect was tantamount to murder: Rumsfeld "tied the hands of commanders while our troops were in contact with the enemy."[16]

Here lies the second preliminary lesson drawn from Iraq and Afghanistan, one that appeals to disgruntled military officers like Batiste, but also to Democrats eager to blame the Bush administration for any and all sins and to neoconservatives looking to absolve themselves of responsibility for botched wars that they had once cavalierly promoted. The corrective to civilian arrogance and misjudgment is obvious: It requires tilting the civil-military balance back in favor of the generals, untying the hands of senior commanders.

From this perspective, the most important lesson to take away from Iraq and Afghanistan is the imperative to empower military professionals. The Petraeus moment of 2007, when all of official Washington from President Bush to the lowest-ranking congressional staffer waited with bated breath for General David Petraeus to formulate basic policy for Iraq, offers a preview of how this lesson might play itself out.

There is also a third perspective, which blames the failures of Iraq and Afghanistan on a problematic relationship between soldiers and society. According to this view, the All-Volunteer Force itself is the problem. As the military historian Adrian Lewis observed, "The most significant transformation in the American conduct of war since World War II and the invention of the atomic bomb was not technological, but cultural, social, and political—*the removal of the American people from the conduct of war.*"[17] Only after 9/11, with the Bush administration waging war on multiple fronts, have the implications of this transformation become fully evident.

A reliance on volunteer-professionals places a de facto cap on the army's overall size. The pool of willing recruits is necessarily limited. Given a choice, most young Americans will opt for opportunities other than military service, with protracted war diminishing rather than enhancing any collective propensity to volunteer. It is virtually inconceivable that any presidential call to the colors, however impassioned, any PR campaign, however cleverly designed, or any package of pay and bonuses, however generous, could reverse this disinclination.

Furthermore, to the extent that an army composed of regulars is no longer a people's army, the people have little say in its use. In effect, the professional military has become an extension of the imperial presidency. The troops fight when and where the commander in chief determines.

Finally, a reliance on professional soldiers eviscerates the concept of civic duty, relieving citizens at large of any obligation to contribute to the nation's defense. Ending the draft during the waning days of the Vietnam War did nothing to heal the divisions created by that conflict; instead, it ratified the separation of army from society. Like mowing lawns and bussing tables, fighting and perhaps dying to sustain the American way of life became something that Americans pay others to do.

So the third lesson of the Iraq War focuses on the need to repair the relationship between army and society. One way to do this is to junk the All-Volunteer Force altogether. Rather than rely on professionals, perhaps it makes sense to revive the tradition of the citizen-soldier.

Proposals to restore this hallowed tradition invariably conjure up images of reinstituting some form of conscription. In place of a system based on the principle of individual choice, those unhappy with the AVF advocate a system based on the principle of state compulsion.

The advantages offered by such a system are hardly trivial. To the extent that Iraq and Afghanistan have exposed the operational, political, and moral problems produced by relying on a small professional force, a draft seems to offer one obvious way to alleviate those problems.

For those who worry that the existing army is overextended, conscription provides a mechanism for expansion. Triple the size of the army—in essence restoring the structure that existed during much of the Cold War—and the personnel shortages that constrain the prosecution of ground campaigns will disappear. Sustaining the military commitment to Iraq for ten or twenty years, or even a century as Senator John McCain and many neoconservatives are willing to contemplate, then becomes a viable proposition.[18]

War planners will no longer find themselves obliged to give short shrift to Contingency A (Afghanistan) in order to support Contingency B (Iraq). The concept of "surge" will take on a whole new meaning with the Pentagon able to dispatch not a measly thirty thousand reinforcements to Iraq or another few thousand to Afghanistan, but one hundred thousand or more additional troops wherever they might be needed. Was the problem with Operation Iraqi Freedom too few "boots on the ground" for occupation and reconstruction? Reconstitute the draft, and that problem goes away.

Creating a mass army might even permit the United States to resuscitate the Weinberger-Powell Doctrine with its emphasis on "overwhelming force."

For those distressed by the absence of a politically meaningful antiwar movement despite the Iraq War's manifest unpopularity, the appeal of conscription differs somewhat. Some political activists look to an Iraq-era draft to do what the Vietnam-era draft did: animate large-scale protest, alter the political dynamic, and eventually shut down any conflict that lacks widespread popular support. The prospect of involuntary service will pry the kids out of the shopping malls and send them into the streets. It will prod the parents of draft-eligible offspring to see politics as something other than a mechanism for doling out entitlements. As a consequence, members of Congress keen to retain their seats will define their wartime responsibilities as something more than simply rubber-stamping spending bills proposed by the White House. In this way, a draft could reinvigorate American democracy, restore the governmental system of checks and balances, and constrain the warmongers inhabiting the executive branch.

For those moved by moral considerations, a draft promises to ensure a more equitable distribution of sacrifice in wartime. No longer will rural Americans, people of color, recent immigrants, and members of the working class fill the ranks of the armed forces in disproportionate numbers. With conscription, the children of the political elite and of the well-to-do will once again bear their fair share of the load. Those reaping the benefits of the American way of life will contribute to its defense, helping to garrison the more distant precincts of empire. Perhaps even the editorial staffs of the *Weekly Standard, National Review,* and the *New Republic* might have the opportunity to serve, a salutary prospect given the propensity of those magazines to argue on behalf of military intervention.

Reconfigure the armed services to fight "small wars"; empower the generals; reconnect soldiering to citizenship— on the surface each of these has a certain appeal. But upon closer examination, each also has large defects. They are the wrong lessons to take from Iraq and Afghanistan.

"Small Wars" for Empire

To begin with, the distinguishing characteristic of "small wars" is not their scope or their duration but their purpose. Great powers wage "small wars" not to defend themselves but to assert control over foreign populations. Denominating an operation "Iraqi Freedom" or "Enduring Freedom" does not alter that reality. Historically, that is, "small wars" are imperial wars. The wars in which the United States currently finds itself engaged are no exception.

In rediscovering "small wars" since 9/11, the American officer corps has also rediscovered a relevant tradition of military literature. Three titles dominate this new "small wars" canon. The first two are French: *Modern Warfare* (1964) by Roger Trinquier and *Counterinsurgency Warfare* (1964) by David Galula. Written by French military professionals, these books synthesize the conclusions drawn from their army's bitter experience following World War II, first in Indochina and then in Algeria. The third title is American in origin: the U.S. Marine Corps' *Small Wars Manual*, published in 1940, but cataloging the marine experience policing the Caribbean during the first third of the twentieth century.[19]

What these three volumes have in common is their imperial context. In the French case, they describe efforts, ultimately futile, to deny subject peoples the right of self-determination. The French army's twofold mission was to restore Indochina to the empire and to sustain the pretense that colonial Algeria—its population 90 percent Arab-speaking and Muslim—formed an integral part of metropolitan France. Both efforts ended in dismal and humiliating failure.

In the American case, the issue differed somewhat. The United States had no particular interest in acquiring Central American or Caribbean colonies.[20] It sought order and access. The mission given to the Marine Corps was to ensure stability in places like Managua and Santo Domingo while requiring adherence to norms devised in Washington and on Wall Street. Yet one need not go as far as Marine Corps Major General Smedley Butler, a veteran of these campaigns, who famously described himself as "a gangster for capitalism," to acknowledge that American purposes were intrinsically imperial. Whereas France sought explicit empire, the United States employed methods that were more oblique and settled for arrangements that were less formal.

Underlying the military's renewed interest in these "small wars" classics is the implicit assumption that the present foretells the future. Among military professionals, the reflexive tendency to assume that the next war will look like the one just concluded, or still under way, has evidently become irresistible. In 1991, high-ranking officers (General Colin Powell not least among them) were sure that Operation Desert Storm had revealed the future of warfare. They were wrong. By 1999, many, like General Wesley Clark, argued that Operation Allied Force, the bombing campaign over Kosovo, provided the template for future operations—wrong again.[21] Undeterred by these misjudgments, senior Pentagon leaders today peer at the horizon and see more insurgencies of the type encountered in Iraq and Afghanistan.

To be sure, if future presidents endorse George W. Bush's imperial ambitions—if, that is, the United States remains committed to achieving in the Greater Middle East during the first third of this century what it did in the Caribbean during the first third of the last century—then the prospect of one, two, many Iraqs becomes plausible. In that event, it probably does make sense to reconfigure U.S. forces to specialize in peacemaking, peacekeeping, and nation-building— contemporary euphemisms for imperial policing.

Yet to assume that wars like Iraq define the military's future evades a larger question: Given what the pursuit of American imperial ambitions in the Greater Middle East has actually produced—not simply since 9/11 but over the course of several decades—why would the United States persist in such a strategy? Instead of changing the military, why not change the policy? Why not pursue more realistic and affordable objectives, abandoning plans to "liberate" (that is, control) the Islamic world—and then configure U.S. forces accordingly?

In other words, the problem with the first lesson of Iraq and Afghanistan—that the Pentagon needs to get better at waging "small wars"—is that it overlooks far more fundamental matters. Rather than transforming the armed forces of the United States into an imperial constabulary, the imperative of the moment is to examine the possibility of devising a nonimperial foreign policy.

Does Knowing Douglas Feith Is Stupid Make Tommy Franks Smart?

Fate has not dealt kindly with the reputations of the policy makers who conceived and promoted the Iraq War. But fate has reserved its cruelest blows for Douglas Feith, who from 2001 to 2005 served as the undersecretary of defense for policy, the third-ranking position in Donald Rumsfeld's Pentagon.

Trained as a lawyer, Feith possessed the temperament of an ideologue. He specialized in enforcing preconceived notions. Rumsfeld felt certain, for example, that Saddam Hussein had links to the 9/11 hijackers. He was also convinced that Saddam had weapons of mass destruction hidden away. Feith's job was to confirm what his boss already knew. Toward that end, he devoted personal attention to the Office of Special Plans (OSP), which duly told Rumsfeld what he wanted to hear. OSP's analysis turned out to be completely wrong, but Feith had accomplished his purpose—and his boss's.

As the countdown toward the invasion proceeded, Rumsfeld didn't want anyone outside of his own shop mucking around with the war planning. The defense secretary found especially irritating concerns expressed by the State Department and some military officers that occupying Iraq might pose some challenges. He counted on Feith to shut out the meddlers and to base Phase IV planning on best-case assumptions. Once again, Feith delivered. Small wonder that Rumsfeld described his subordinate as "a rare talent."[22] Rumsfeld had every reason to be satisfied.

Yet Rumsfeld's assessment seems unlikely to stand. Whatever Feith may achieve during the remainder of his life and whatever epitaph he chooses for inscription on his gravestone, history will remember him as "the stupidest fucking guy on the planet."

The source of that judgment, which is likely to remain definitive, is General Tommy Franks.[23] As commander of U.S. Central Command (CENTCOM) from 2000 to 2003,

Franks planned and directed the successive invasions of Afghanistan and then Iraq. When he retired from active service soon after the fall of Baghdad, Franks was unquestionably the nation's best known senior military officer, achieving for a time something akin to celebrity status. He was also, at least briefly, highly respected—the commander who had, in rapid succession, won two supposedly decisive victories. At a 2004 White House ceremony during which he awarded Franks the Presidential Medal of Freedom, George W. Bush praised the general as a "brilliant strategist." In Afghanistan, Franks had "defeated the Taliban in just a few short weeks." In Iraq, he had "defeated Saddam Hussein's regime and reached Baghdad in less than a month." As a result, the president continued, "Today the people of Iraq and Afghanistan are building a secure and permanent democratic future." Bush declared that Franks would carry into history the title "liberator."[24]

That same year, Franks published a memoir, which became an instant bestseller. The chief purpose of *American Soldier* was to flesh out the heroic story that President Bush had outlined, securing in perpetuity the general's reputation as a Great Captain as well as the chief architect of two historic victories. Franks emerges from the pages of his own account as the central figure in Bush's liberation narrative.

Here lies the context for the lambasting that Franks ministered to Feith—and for his antipathy toward other would-be competitors for the victor's laurels. *American Soldier* was an exercise in score-settling. Although Franks spared President Bush direct criticism—he depicted the commander in chief as something between an amiable cheerleader and a passive bystander—few others got off so lightly. The general mocked "the intellectual arrogance" of civilian officials back in Washington, who imagined that air power alone "could kick open a door, through which exiled Iraqi opposition groups would march triumphantly to liberate their country." He dismissed White House terrorism czar Richard Clarke as an impractical blowhard. Secretary of Defense Donald Rumsfeld came off as a difficult boss whom Franks patiently struggled to manage. Nor did Franks spare his fellow professionals. He savaged serving members of the Joint Chiefs of Staff as bureaucratic "motherfuckers," whose advice amounted to little more than "parochial bullshit."[25]

In short, when it came to Iraq and Afghanistan, Franks wanted to clear up any doubt about who was in charge: He was, from start to finish. The invasion plans were his plans, reflecting his own conception of how to wage such campaigns. From 9/11 onward, according to Franks, CENTCOM " 'pushed strategy up,' rather than waiting for Washington to 'push tactics down.' "[26]

So the second emerging lesson of Iraq and Afghanistan—emphasizing the need to give senior military leaders a free hand—runs into an immediate problem: The general who directed each of those wars during its formative stage says that, at every step along the way, the crucial decisions were his. Civilian meddling wasn't a problem because Franks refused to let the civilians meddle. "My name is not Westmoreland," he growled during the Afghan campaign, referring to the general who commanded U.S. forces in Vietnam, "and I'm not going to go along with Washington giving tactics and targets to our kids in the cockpits and on the ground."[27]

It follows that if things began falling apart soon after U.S. forces occupied Baghdad, as they manifestly did, then responsibility lies with the individual giving the orders. Blaming Washington alone won't do. If the forces invading Iraq in March 2003 did so without a clear-cut plan for occupying the country, then, by his own account, primary responsibility for that oversight rests with the overall military commander. If that planning failure created the conditions from which an insurgency evolved, again the primary fault necessarily lies with the commander.

Unless *American Soldier* is a lie, to blame civilian officials like Rumsfeld, Wolfowitz, and Feith for the chaos that became Iraq is to commit a grave injustice. They were not calling the shots. Tommy Franks was. In such circumstances, to give Franks a pass is to abandon a core principle of the military profession in which commanders are explicitly charged with responsibility for everything that their troops do or fail to do.

Yet to single out Franks alone for his lapses, no matter how egregious, would be unfair. His failures in Iraq—and in Afghanistan, where his claim that the Taliban had been "squeeze[d] into extinction" turned out to be wildly premature[28]—are symptomatic of a much more widespread phenomenon: When it comes to reaping political advantage from our supposed military superiority, Americans have been getting a lousy return on their investment.

One consistently overlooked explanation for this phenomenon is that the quality of American generalship since the end of the Cold War has seldom risen above the mediocre. Although the overall quality of U.S. forces may be at an all-time high, the same cannot be said of the most recent generation of four-star generals and admirals.

This is one of those dirty little secrets to which the world's only superpower has yet to own up. As the United States has come to rely ever more heavily on armed force to prop up its position of global preeminence, the quality of senior American military leadership has been consistently disappointing. The troops are ever willing, the technology remarkable, but first-rate generalship has been hard to come by.

Considering recent military history, the problem has not been that high-ranking commanders have lacked authority, as Batiste and other disgruntled officers contend. In fact, civilian policy makers have allowed senior commanders wide latitude in the planning and conduct of operations. The problem is that the generals have not used their authority wisely.

Evidence to sustain this charge is available in abundance. It begins with Operation Desert Storm, a supposedly historic victory marred by two critical failures. First, U.S. forces permitted the Iraqi Republican Guard, the mainstay of Saddam Hussein's army, to escape destruction. Second, the cease-fire negotiated at Safwan on March 1, 1991, allowed the dictator all the wiggle room he needed to suppress an uprising by Saddam's internal opponents. These lapses stemmed directly from errors in judgment by the field commander, H. Norman Schwarzkopf, with General Colin Powell, then chairman of the Joint Chiefs, running interference. As a result, Saddam preserved his hold on power and U.S. forces remained to garrison the Persian Gulf, with consequences that proved to be deeply problematic.[29]

Errors in generalship, albeit on a smaller scale, marred the humanitarian intervention in Somalia that began the following year. Disregarding basic principles of security and the requirement for unity of command, American commanders given the mission of eliminating the warlord Mohammed Farah Aidid instead blundered into a trap he had set. Although subsequently enshrined as a heroic episode, the famous Mogadishu firefight possessed little immediate significance. Yet this minor tactical setback caused Clinton administration policy in Somalia to collapse, a failure interpreted by Osama bin Laden as evidence of American weakness.

Back in Washington, the search for a scapegoat began almost immediately. Critics fastened on Secretary of Defense Les Aspin as the designated fall guy. Soon thereafter, he lost his job. Yet the real explanation for this miniature catastrophe was that senior commanders on the ground, Major General Thomas Montgomery and Major General William Garrison, had misread and badly underestimated their adversary. As a result, they set their own troops up for defeat.[30] Once again, maladroit generalship helped pave the way for much bigger problems to come.

Then there was Operation Allied Force, the 1999 NATO air campaign over Kosovo, designed and directed by NATO's supreme commander, General Wesley Clark. Contemporary accounts portrayed Kosovo as "Albright's War," the product of diplomatic miscalculation on the part of Secretary of State Madeleine Albright. Yet Kosovo was equally "Clark's War."

The immediate political issue was whether or not the province of Kosovo should remain part of Serbia. Insisting that it would, the Serb dictator Slobodan Milošević was employing heavy-handed methods to suppress Kosovar Albanian separatists. For Clark, larger considerations hovered in the background. He saw Kosovo as an opportunity to demonstrate NATO's continuing relevance in a post–Cold War world and to validate his own pet theory of coercive diplomacy, "using forces, not force," to achieve political objectives.[31] Clark expected threats alone to suffice: A properly designed display of superior power would persuade his adversary to give way, making it unnecessary actually to pull the trigger.

So Clark set out to orchestrate a showdown with

Milošević, confident of achieving a neat, tidy, and bloodless outcome. "I know Milosevic," Clark assured officials back in Washington, "he doesn't want to get bombed."[32]

When Milošević proceeded to call Clark's bluff, NATO found itself in a shooting war. Clark expected three or four days of air attacks to bring the Serbs to their knees. Again, he erred. Milošević had his own surprise in store: An intensified campaign of ethnic cleansing in Kosovo created a huge refugee crisis that caught Clark unawares. Meanwhile, the NATO bombing campaign dragged on. By the time it finally ended seventy-eight days later, an armada of 829 combat aircraft had flown some 38,000 sorties while expending over 28,000 weapons. NATO bombs had killed an estimated 500 civilians. Clark's concept of "using forces, not force," hadn't worked. Soon thereafter, the general found himself hustled briskly into early retirement.[33]

The point of rehearsing this chronicle of misjudgment and miscalculation is simply this: The shortcomings evident in the way that General Tommy Franks planned and executed his two wars were hardly unique. They form part of a pattern. Time and again since the end of the Cold War, senior military officers shouldering the challenge of wartime command have been found wanting.

In Iraq, after Franks surrendered the reins of command, that pattern continued. When he arrived in Baghdad in 2003, Lieutenant General Ricardo Sanchez inherited a brewing insurgency. His efforts to suppress that insurgency produced the opposite effect: Conditions worsened, helped along by the Abu Ghraib scandal that detonated on Sanchez's watch. In 2004, General George Casey succeeded Sanchez and presided over Iraq's gradual descent into something like full-fledged civil war. Not only did Sanchez and Casey fail to accomplish their assigned mission; as a result of their efforts, mission accomplishment actually became a more distant prospect.

When General David Petraeus succeeded Casey in February 2007, he arrived bearing a freshly updated counterinsurgency doctrine and the promise of thirty thousand temporary reinforcements. During Petraeus's tenure, violence in Iraq subsided—in considerable part because coalition forces began accommodating Sunni tribal leaders who numbered among the most fervent opponents of the U.S.-installed Iraqi government. Bribes and guns helped turn the Sunnis against their erstwhile Al Qaeda allies. It was the cops paying the Crips to take on the Bloods.

Observers hailed Petraeus's achievements. By 2008, as Operation Iraqi Freedom entered its sixth year, the general had managed to get the war off the front pages of major American newspapers. Yet, however welcome this was to the Bush administration politically, substantive improvements remained limited. The pacification of Iraq remained a distant hope. "Success" amounted to a stabilized stalemate, likely to absorb the attention of U.S. forces for years to come.

The bottom line is this: Civilian meddling, however objectionable, cannot fully explain the disappointing results achieved by U.S. forces since the Cold War ended two decades ago. Allegations that senior commanders from Schwarzkopf to Petraeus have labored under unreasonable constraints are unsustainable. Granted an abundance of resources and considerable autonomy, the generals simply haven't gotten the job done. War is a difficult business, and to question the good intentions of any of these officers would be unfair. No doubt each did his level best. Yet, in one instance after another, senior commanders have performed less well than the troops in their charge.

"At the summit," Winston Churchill once observed,

"true politics and strategy are one."[34] The essential function of the general-in-chief is to preserve that unity, achieving victories that advance the larger purposes of the state, however imperfectly articulated by civilian authorities. Great Captains make armed force purposeful. They harmonize war and politics.

The American military tradition includes such figures. During his tenure as commander of the Continental Army, George Washington was one. So, too, during the Civil War was Ulysses S. Grant, ably assisted by his chief lieutenant, William T. Sherman. Arguably, in their direction of the war against Nazi Germany, the team of George C. Marshall, as army chief of staff, and Dwight D. Eisenhower, as Allied commander in Europe, might stand in the same company.

The post–Cold War era, as measured by the number of alarms, excursions, and interventions perhaps the busiest period in all of U.S. military history, has seen no one even remotely of this caliber. The senior officers exercising wartime command during that period have not lacked authority. They have lacked ability.

Why the Draft Is Not a Good Idea and Won't Happen

This brings us to the third of the Iraq War's ostensible lessons: closing the divide between the army and society by scrapping the All-Volunteer Force and reverting to conscription.

There are several reasons why the draft is a bad idea. For one thing, a large draftee army is unaffordable. The Pentagon is currently planning to expand U.S. ground forces by ninety-two thousand over the next several years. The Congressional Budget Office estimates the price tag for this modest increase at $108 billion.[35] To train, equip, and sustain the current active-duty force and to defray the costs of ongoing operations, the Pentagon is currently spending approximately $700 billion per year. Doubling the size of that force to three million—less than 1 percent of the total population, yet sufficiently large to make a "small wars" imperial strategy sustainable—would require an annual defense budget upwards of a trillion dollars. Even if the bodies needed to fill such a force exist, the money doesn't.

Nor does the military want those bodies, except on very specific terms. Toward the end of the Vietnam War when Richard Nixon first proposed abolishing the draft, the Joint Chiefs of Staff opposed the idea. Since then, with the partial exception of the Marine Corps, each of the services has become enamored with a force composed of highly skilled, long-service "warriors." When Secretary of Defense Donald Rumsfeld dismissed the draftees of prior wars as having added "no value, no advantage, really," he may have violated some canon of political correctness, but he accurately reflected prevailing Pentagon opinion.[36] The truth is that the four-star generals and admirals view citizen-soldiers as more trouble than they're worth.

As for the hope that reinstituting conscription might reenergize politics, it's akin to the notion that putting Christ back in Christmas will reawaken American spirituality. A pleasant enough fantasy, it overlooks the forces that transformed a religious holiday into an orgy of consumption in the first place.

Crediting President Nixon with ending the draft is like tagging Macy's for commercializing the birth of Jesus—it ignores the backstory. The fact is that when Nixon pulled the plug on selective service, the system was already on life support. The American people killed the draft. In the midst

of a misbegotten war, they withdrew from the federal government its hitherto widely accepted prerogative of commanding citizens to serve. For his own cynical reasons—he
hoped to deflate the antiwar movement—Nixon acceded to
this popular demand. One serendipitous result was to lay
the basis for a new consensus, henceforth defining military
service as a matter of individual choice. In short order, liberals, conservatives, and centrists all signed on, and the bargain became permanent.

For a brief moment in the immediate aftermath of 9/11,
President Bush might have revisited that consensus. Arguably, he could have proposed a new civil-military bargain
that would have spread the burden of military service more
broadly across American society. Perhaps anticipating that a
"people's army" might limit his own freedom of action,
Bush instead affirmed the existing arrangement. Since then,
his administration's extraordinary blunders, especially in
Iraq, have made that bargain all but sacrosanct. In effect, the
global war on terror has revived the Vietnam-era street wisdom that politicians are either callous or stupid and will
sacrifice the lives of young Americans rather than owning
up to the consequences of their misjudgments. Whatever
the threat posed by Al Qaeda, most parents with teenagers
will view the prospect of a draft as posing a greater immediate danger to their children's well-being.

So whatever the theoretical appeal of using the draft to
draw Americans out of their torpor and nudge the Congress
into doing its job, politically it's just not in the cards. Today,
with the possible exception of conservative evangelicals, no
significant segment of the electorate will concede to the federal government the authority to order their sons and
daughters into uniform. Legislation mandating involuntary
service would almost certainly elicit the same reaction that

Prohibition induced back in the 1920s, only more quickly and on a larger scale: The law would be unenforceable.

Granted, arguments that a draft might correct the inequities inherent in our existing military system have indisputable merit. To anyone with a conscience, sending soldiers back to Iraq or Afghanistan for multiple combat tours while the rest of the country chills out can hardly seem an acceptable arrangement. It is unfair, unjust, and morally corrosive.

Yet seldom in American history have questions of fairness or equitability played a decisive role in shaping public policy. The present moment does not qualify as one of those occasions; if it were, we would not tolerate the gaping disparities between rich and poor in our society. Relying on a small number of volunteers to bear the burden of waging an open-ended global war might make Americans uneasy, but uneasiness will not suffice to produce change. To salve the nation's conscience, the government might augment our hard-pressed troops with pricey contractor-mercenaries, but it won't actually trouble citizens to do anything. Indeed, the privatization of war—evident in the prominence achieved by armies-for-rent such as the notorious Blackwater—suggests a tacit willingness to transform military service from a civic function into an economic enterprise, with money rather than patriotism the motive. Americans may not like mercenaries, but many of them harbor an even greater dislike for the prospect of sending their loved ones to fight in some godforsaken country on the other side of the world.

In short, although conscription will continue to make a nice topic for angry op-eds and heartfelt letters-to-the-editor, the chances of Congress actually enacting legislation to restore the draft are nil. In this instance, the views of

Congress reflect the views of the American people. Whatever its shortcomings, the professional army created after Vietnam is here to stay.

The Enduring Nature of War

If gearing up to fight "small wars," deferring to the brass, and scrapping the All-Volunteer Force are the wrong lessons to be drawn from our recent military experience, then what are the right ones?

Lurking behind this simple question are several larger ones. How is it that our widely touted post–Cold War military supremacy has produced not enhanced security but the prospect of open-ended conflict? Why is it that when we flex our muscles on behalf of peace and freedom, the world beyond our borders becomes all the more cantankerous and disorderly? To turn Madeleine Albright's famous question to Colin Powell on its head, what exactly is the point of using this superb army of ours if the result is Iraq and Afghanistan?

The events of the recent past offer several lessons that illuminate these questions. The first, and perhaps most important, concerns the nature of war. Iraq and Afghanistan remind us that war is not subject to reinvention, whatever George W. Bush and Pentagon proponents of the so-called Revolution in Military Affairs or "shock-and-awe" may contend.

War's essential nature is fixed, permanent, intractable, and irrepressible. War's constant companions are uncertainty and risk. "War is the realm of chance," wrote the military theorist Carl von Clausewitz nearly two centuries ago. "No other human activity gives it greater scope: no other has such incessant and varied dealings with this intruder," a judgment that the invention of the computer, the Internet, and precision-guided munitions has done nothing to overturn.[37] "The statesman who yields to war fever," Churchill correctly observed, "is no longer the master of policy, but the slave of unforeseeable and uncontrollable events."[38] Therefore, any notion that innovative techniques and new technologies will subject war to definitive human direction is simply whimsical.

These ancient truths, repeatedly affirmed over the course of centuries, are so commonplace as to be clichés. Yet since the end of the Cold War, and especially during the first several years of the global war on terror, American political leaders, along with more than a few high-ranking military officers, have behaved as if they had become obsolete—or at least no longer applied to the United States.

To appreciate the folly to which such military thinkers fell prey, one need look no further than the lowly IED—the Improvised Explosive Device, or roadside bomb, that has proven such a nemesis of U.S. forces in Iraq and, to a lesser extent, Afghanistan.

The high-tech forces invading those two countries were oblivious to the potential threat posed by these homemade bombs. The tempo of operations was expected to render the enemy unable to move or even think, much less fabricate deadly new weapons. A small force, equipped with a high-tech arsenal, enjoying the advantages of information superiority, and closing on its objective at a breakneck pace, would dictate the terms of combat. The drive on Baghdad in April 2003 seemed to validate this concept. "The speed of the advance was so dramatic it unhinged the enemy," exulted General Jack Keane, the army's vice chief of staff.[39]

An electronically enhanced ability to see, analyze, decide,

and act quickly had seemingly provided U.S. forces with an insurmountable advantage. Shortly after the Iraqi capital fell, Vice Admiral Arthur Cebrowski summarized the argument: "Speed matters. Speed kills. It leads to less collateral damage and fewer U.S. casualties." Speed was enabling U.S. forces to do more with less. "Speed is force enhancement," Marine General Peter Pace, then vice chairman of the Joint Chiefs of Staff, chimed in. "If you can deliver five divisions anywhere in the world in 90 days, might you have the same impact by getting three divisions there in 30 days?"[40]

A smaller, more agile force could also accomplish a wider range of tasks. The rationale for launching Operation Iraqi Freedom in 2003 with fewer troops than were used for Operation Desert Storm in 1991, explained Douglas Feith, "was strategic and goes far beyond Iraq." The upper echelons of the Defense Department were counting on the smaller invasion force to discredit the notion that "the United States should not do anything without hundreds of thousands of troops." The problem with that "old way of thinking," continued Feith, was that it "makes our military less usable."[41] During the opening years of the twenty-first century, the Pentagon convinced itself that it had discovered a formula—technologically enhanced speed yielding both operational and political certainty—that was making force "usable" as never before.

The IED—which can be built for about the cost of a pizza—brought the American victory express to a crashing halt.[42] As the insurgent weapon of choice, it denied U.S. forces the decisive outcome thought to have been gained by the fall of Saddam Hussein. Having gotten in quickly enough, the Americans found that they couldn't get out. Liberation gave way to occupation. Speed was no longer a war winner. Persistent presence became the new imperative.

As had the Germans in Yugoslavia, the Soviets in Afghanistan, and the Israelis on the West Bank, the Americans in
Iraq now discovered that apparent strengths only exposed
new vulnerabilities.

Forces optimized for mobility found themselves tethered
to a network of roads and fixed bases. Rather than the rapid
dash, the signature of U.S. operations became the checkpoint,
the traffic stop, and the dismounted patrol. For the insurgents, targeting the Americans proved to be a fairly simple
proposition. For the Americans, identifying, much less locating, the insurgents posed a more daunting challenge.

In crucial respects, despite all the emphasis on quickness, U.S. forces proved far less agile than their adversaries.
The introduction of the IED touched off an intense competition. To defeat this unanticipated threat, the Department of
Defense has invested well over $10 billion (with more to
come), hoping to provide its soldiers with better protection
and a better ability to identify and disarm bombs.[43] Meanwhile, insurgent bomb makers, despite a comparative
scarcity of resources, have continually upgraded IED lethality while coming up with ever better ways to conceal and
trigger the increasingly lethal devices. As measured by the
continuing toll of IED-related U.S. casualties, the insurgents
consistently outperformed the Pentagon in this contest.[44]

The implications proved to be strategic as well as tactical.
Tied down by IED-equipped insurgents, U.S. forces could
not attend to other looming threats. The arena of President
Bush's "global war" narrowed in scope, being largely con-
fined to Iraq and Afghanistan. The remaining members of
his "axis of evil" got a pass. Iran, one member of that axis,
actually gained influence and stature.

So the first lesson to be taken away from the Bush administration's two military adventures is simply this: War

remains today what it has always been—elusive, untamed, costly, difficult to control, fraught with surprise, and sure to give rise to unexpected consequences. Only the truly demented will imagine otherwise.

The Limited Utility of Force

The second lesson of Iraq and Afghanistan derives from the first. As has been the case throughout history, the utility of armed force remains finite. Even in the information age, to the extent that force "works," it does so with respect to a limited range of contingencies.

This lesson bears directly on the ambitions that inform present-day American statecraft.

Over the course of the Cold War, force emerged as a favored instrument of U.S. policy. Writing in 1958, Niebuhr had worried about Americans becoming "strangely enamored with military might." The outcome of the Cold War did nothing to ease that infatuation. After 9/11, Washington's affinity for coercion reached new heights. For President Bush, the "military option" has always remained "on the table." His administration has treated military power as an all-purpose tool, no longer to be employed as a last resort or exclusively for defensive purposes. Rather, armed force has offered the means to set things right and to fix whatever is broken.

Time and again, for example, President Bush insisted that in Iraq, the United States was fighting not simply to protect itself or its interests, but to ensure the spread of democracy and human rights. There were two ways to interpret this so-called freedom agenda. The first interpretation took the president's words at face value: He saw war as a vehicle for deliverance and liberation. Through violence, either threatened or employed outright, the United States aimed to bring entire nations into conformity with Western, liberal values. This was Bush channeling Woodrow Wilson via Paul Wolfowitz.

The alternative was to see the freedom agenda as purely cynical, providing a tissue of moral legitimacy to a strategy of naked aggression. Here, the belief was that force would produce hegemony. Coercion, starting with Iraq (but not ending there), would enable the United States to subjugate the Greater Middle East. This was Bush channeling Theodore Roosevelt, as interpreted by Dick Cheney.

Whether Bush himself leaned toward the militant idealism of Wilson and Wolfowitz or the militant nationalism of TR and Cheney may well be a moot point. In his own mind, the two schools in all likelihood merged. Bush would hardly be the first U.S. president for whom the axiom "America fights for freedom" served simultaneously as core conviction and convenient rationale.

The real point is that whether the United States has been attempting to liberate or to dominate, events in Iraq and Afghanistan suggest that the effort is not working. Armed force wielded by the United States will neither free the peoples of the Greater Middle East nor put this country in a position to control the region. We are playing a losing hand.

In Iraq, the Bush administration acquired a ramshackle, ungovernable, and unresponsive dependency that, five years after the overthrow of Saddam Hussein, remained incapable of securing its own borders or managing its own affairs. A nation-building project launched with confident predictions of repeating the successes achieved in Germany and Japan after 1945 instead compares unfavorably with the federal government's response to Hurricane Katrina. By the end of 2007, Iraqi electrical generation still met barely half of daily national requirements. Baghdad households were receiving power an average of twelve hours each day—six hours fewer than when the Baathists ruled.[45] Oil production had still not returned to preinvasion levels.[46] Reports of widespread fraud, waste, and sheer ineptitude in the administration of U.S. aid had become so commonplace that they barely lasted a news cycle.[47]

Meanwhile, Bush administration officials repeatedly complained—to little avail—about the squabbling that paralyzed the Iraqi parliament and the rampant corruption that engulfed Iraqi ministries. If a primary function of government is to provide services, the government of Iraq could hardly be said to exist. By comparison, Nicaragua under the Somozas or the Philippines under Ferdinand Marcos qualified as models of good governance.

Many of the same judgments apply to Afghanistan. With liberation, that nation quickly reclaimed its status as the world's leading producer of illegal drugs, by 2007 providing a staggering 93 percent of the heroin, morphine, and other opiates on the world market.[48] The U.S.-installed government of Afghanistan remained weak and inadequate. Reflecting the limits of his actual writ, Afghan president Hamid Karzai acquired the sardonic title "mayor of Kabul." Meanwhile, the Taliban proved stubbornly resilient. Although no official name change occurred, Operation Enduring Freedom tacitly became Operation Enduring Obligation. For Washington, the chief good news out of Afghanistan was that here at least the United States was not alone: NATO shared the burden of propping up the new order, such as it was. Yet under even the most optimistic scenario, Western forces will remain stuck in Afghanistan for many years, if not decades, to come.

Although die-hard supporters of the global war on terror will insist otherwise, events in Iraq and Afghanistan have demonstrated definitively that further reliance on coercive methods will not enable the United States to achieve its objectives. Whether the actual aim is to democratize the Islamic world or subdue it, the military "option" is not the answer.

In this regard, the lesson that the two wars offer is one that Americans once grasped intuitively. As the novelist and World War II veteran Norman Mailer put it, "Fighting a war to fix something works about as good as going to a whorehouse to get rid of a clap."[49] As a problem solver, war leaves much to be desired.

The Folly of Preventive War

The Bush Doctrine itself provides the basis for a third lesson. For centuries, the Western moral tradition has categorically rejected the concept of *preventive war.* The events of 9/11 convinced some that this tradition no longer applied. Overriding security concerns supposedly imposed a higher moral obligation to act. Old constraints had to give way. Yet our actual experience with preventive war suggests that, even setting moral considerations aside, to launch a war today to eliminate a danger that *might* pose a threat at some future date is just plain stupid. It doesn't work.

The Bush administration has entertained a different view. According to the "one percent doctrine," to prevent any recurrence of 9/11, even the slightest prospect of an attack requires prompt anticipatory action.[50] In a 2002 commencement address delivered at West Point, President Bush explained why. The events of 9/11, he said, had thoroughly discredited the Cold War concepts of *containment* and *deterrence.* Henceforth, the United States needed to snuff out threats before they could materialize. "In the world we have entered," the president concluded, "the only path to safety

is the path of action."[51] Bush vowed to act. Simply put, the
United States had arrogated to itself—and to itself alone—
an unlimited first-strike prerogative.

Here again, the counsel of Reinhold Niebuhr deserves
careful consideration. The early days of the Cold War had
produced its own version of the "one percent doctrine."
When the Soviet Union broke the U.S. nuclear monopoly in
1949, it appeared in some quarters to be only a matter of
time before Americans would face the choice of being either
"Red or dead." The country could avoid that choice by putting its hard-earned strategic superiority to work immediately, before it withered away. Here lay the rationale for a
first strike against Russia: By attacking the Soviets before
they could build up a large nuclear arsenal, the United
States in one fell swoop could eliminate its rival and achieve
permanent peace and security.

Niebuhr regarded this line of reasoning with horror.
"The idea of a preventive war," he wrote, tempts those eager
"to pick the most propitious moment for the start of what
they regard as inevitable hostilities." Yet he went on to say
that "the rest of us must resist such ideas with every moral
resource." In Niebuhr's judgment, the concept of *preventive
war* failed both normatively and pragmatically. Not only
was it morally wrong; it was also mad. "Nothing in history
is inevitable," he observed, "including the probable. So long
as war has not broken out, we still have the possibility of
avoiding it. Those who think that there is little difference
between a cold and a hot war are either knaves or fools."[52]

Throughout the second half of the twentieth century,
such cautionary views, shared by American presidents,
helped avoid a nuclear conflagration. Between 2002 and
2003, they did not suffice to carry the day. In Iraq, the knaves
and fools got their war.

Yet a military operation expected to demonstrate the efficacy of preventive war accomplished just the reverse. The looming threat that ostensibly made the invasion of Iraq an urgent necessity—Saddam's weapons of mass destruction—proved to be nonexistent. The war's promised outcome proved elusive. Its costs turned out to be far greater than anyone in the administration had anticipated.

History has repeatedly demonstrated the irrationality of preventive war. If the world needed a further demonstration, President Bush provided it. Iraq shows us why the Bush Doctrine was a bad idea in the first place and why its abrogation has become essential. For principled guidance in determining when the use of force is appropriate, the country should conform to the Just War tradition—not only because that tradition is consistent with our professed moral values, but also because its provisions provide an eminently useful guide for sound statecraft.

The Lost Art of Strategy

Finally, there is a fourth lesson, relating to the formulation of strategy. The results of U.S. policy in Iraq and Afghanistan suggest that in the upper echelons of the government and among the senior ranks of the officer corps, this has become a lost art.

Since the end of the Cold War, the tendency among civilians—with President Bush a prime example—has been to confuse strategy with ideology. The president's freedom agenda, which supposedly provided a blueprint for how to prosecute the global war on terror, expressed grandiose aspirations without serious effort to assess the means required to achieve them.

Since the Vietnam War ended, the tendency among military officers has been to confuse strategy with operations. No one illustrates this inclination more vividly than does Tommy Franks, thanks in large part to the gift of his revealing memoir.

Although for public consumption Franks cultivated a self-deprecating, country-boy persona—the kid from West Texas professing amazement at how far he'd come—Franks actually considered himself an erudite student of his profession and an original thinker. During his rise through the ranks, he "had read about both war and peace: the accumulated wisdom of Sun Tzu and Clausewitz, Bertram [sic] Russell and Gandhi."[53]

Although Franks sprinkled his tale with quotations from long-deceased Chinese and German philosophers, his own observations never rise above the pedestrian. When first directed to plan the invasion of Iraq, for example, Franks sat down, legal pad in hand, and sketched out his "template" for decisive victory. The resulting matrix, which *American Soldier* proudly reprints in its original handwritten form, consisted of seven horizontal "lines of operation"—enumerating U.S. capabilities—intersecting with nine vertical "slices," each describing a source of Saddam Hussein's hold on power. At select points of intersection—thirty-six in all—Franks drew a "starburst." According to Franks, these "lines and slices" offered an exquisitely designed example of what he termed "basic *grand strategy*."[54]

Yet even a casual examination of Franks's matrix shows that it did not remotely approximate a strategy. For starters, it was devoid of political context. Narrowly focused on the upcoming fight, it paid no attention to the aftermath. Defining the problem as Iraq alone, it ignored other regional power relationships and made no provision for how war might alter those relationships, whether for good or for ill. It was completely ahistorical and made no reference to culture, religion, or ethnic identity. It had no moral dimension. It failed even to include a statement of purpose.

Here we come face-to-face with the essential dilemma with which the United States has unsuccessfully wrestled since the Soviets deprived us of a stabilizing adversary—a dilemma that the events of 9/11 only served to intensify. The political elite that ought to bear the chief responsibility for crafting grand strategy instead nurses fantasies of either achieving permanent global hegemony or remaking the world in America's image. Meanwhile, the military elite that could puncture those fantasies and help restore a modicum of realism to U.S. policy fixates on campaigns and battles, with generalship largely a business of organizing and coordinating matériel.

Determined to preclude any interference from insufferable civilians like Douglas Feith and to reconstitute war as the exclusive province of military professionals, self-described warriors like Tommy Franks studiously disregard either political purpose or potential political complications. Never having forgiven Secretary of Defense Robert McNamara for Vietnam, Franks and other soldiers of his generation instinctively view civilians as troublemakers, constantly straying onto turf that is rightfully their own. Averting such unwelcome encroachments constitutes a categorical imperative.

Reasserting a professional monopoly over the conduct of warfare requires drawing the brightest possible line between politics and war, thereby preventing civilian and military considerations from becoming entangled. Hence, the senior commander who (like Franks) experiences combat vicariously in the comfort of an air-conditioned headquarters nonetheless insists on styling himself a "warfighter."

He does so for more than merely symbolic reasons. Assuming that identity permits him to assert prerogatives to which the officer corps now adamantly lays absolute claim.

As if by default, getting to Baghdad (or Kabul) becomes war's primary—almost its sole—purpose. The result is war undertaken in an atmosphere of astonishing strategic naïveté, leading soldiers like Franks and civilians like Feith to assume that, with a couple of quick battlefield victories, everything else will simply fall into place.

Fighting is, of course, integral to war. But in ways not always appreciated by, or even agreeable to, those who actually pull triggers and drop bombs, war is also, and always, inherently political. Indeed, if war is to have any conceivable justification or utility, it must remain subordinated to politics. Effecting that subordination lies at the very heart of strategy.

Many factors have contributed to the military crisis in which the United States finds itself today: greed, envy, miscalculation, ideological blinders, the nature of the international system, the sins of past generations coming due, the hubris of militarized civilians, the iron law of unintended consequences. All of these deserve mention. But in *American Soldier* we see on vivid display one additional factor: an approach to generalship that misconstrues the very purpose of war.

The four lessons of Iraq and Afghanistan boil down to this: Events have exposed as illusory American pretensions to having mastered war. Even today war is hardly more subject to human control than the tides or the weather. Simply trying harder—investing ever larger sums in even more advanced technology, devising novel techniques, or even improving the quality of American generalship—will not enable the United States to evade that reality.

By extension, the presumption of U.S. military supremacy that achieved such broad currency during the years following the Cold War is completely spurious. The exercise of military power will not enable the United States to evade the predicament to which the crisis of profligacy has given rise. To persist in following that path is to invite inevitable overextension, bankruptcy, and ruin.

As measured by results achieved, the performance of the military since the end of the Cold War and especially since 9/11 has been unimpressive. This indifferent record of success leads some observers, especially neoconservatives, to argue that we need a bigger army or a different army, necessarily implying yet another hefty increase in defense spending.

But the problem lies less with the army that we have—a very fine one, which every citizen should wish to preserve—than with the requirements that we have imposed on our soldiers. Rather than expanding or reforming that army, we need to treat it with the respect that it deserves. That means protecting it from further abuse of the sort that it has endured since 2001.

America doesn't need a bigger army. It needs a smaller—that is, more modest—foreign policy, one that assigns soldiers missions that are consistent with their capabilities. Modesty implies giving up on the illusions of grandeur to which the end of the Cold War and then 9/11 gave rise. It also means reining in the imperial presidents who expect the army to make good on those illusions. When it comes to supporting the troops, here lies the essence of a citizen's obligation.

Conclusion:
The Limits of Power

Victorious in snowy Iowa, the candidate proclaimed—to wild applause—that "our time for change has come." If elected president, he vowed to break the power of the lobbyists, provide affordable health care for all, cut middle-class taxes, end both the war in Iraq and the nation's dependence on foreign oil, and "unite America and the world against the common threats of the twenty-first century." In an earlier age, aspirants for the highest office in the land ventured to promise a chicken in every pot. In the present age, candidates like Senator Barack Obama set their sights on tackling "terrorism and nuclear weapons, climate change and poverty, genocide and disease."

The agenda is an admirable one. Yet to imagine that installing a particular individual in the Oval Office will produce decisive action on any of these fronts is to succumb to the grandest delusion of all. The quadrennial ritual of electing (or reelecting) a president is not an exercise in promoting change, regardless of what candidates may claim and ordinary voters believe. The real aim is to ensure continuity, to keep intact the institutions and arrangements that define present-day Washington. The veterans of past administrations who sign on as campaign advisers are not interested in curbing the bloated powers of the presidency. They want to share in exercising those powers. The retired generals and admirals who line up behind their preferred candidate don't want to dismantle the national security state. They want to preserve and, if possible, expand it. The candidates who decry the influence of money in national politics are among those most skilled at courting the well-heeled to amass millions in campaign contributions.

No doubt the race for the presidency matters. It just doesn't matter nearly as much as the media's obsessive coverage suggests. Whoever moves into the White House on January 20, 2009, the fundamental problem facing the country—a yawning disparity between what Americans expect and what they are willing or able to pay—will remain stubbornly in place. Any presidential initiatives aimed at alleviating the crisis of profligacy, reforming our political system, or devising a more realistic military policy are likely, at best, to have a marginal effect.

Paradoxically, the belief that all (or even much) will be well, if only the right person assumes the reins as president and commander in chief serves to underwrite the status quo. Counting on the next president to fix whatever is broken promotes expectations of easy, no-cost cures, permitting ordinary citizens to absolve themselves of responsibility for the nation's predicament. The same Americans who profess to despise all that Washington represents look to—depending on partisan affiliation—a new John F. Kennedy or a new Ronald Reagan to set things right again. Rather than seeing the imperial presidency as part of the problem, they persist in the fantasy that a chief executive, given a clear mandate, will "change" the way Washington works and restore the nation to good health. Yet to judge by the performance of presidents over the past half century, including both Kennedy and Reagan (whose legacies are far more mixed than their supporters will acknowledge), a citizenry that looks to the White House for deliverance is assured of disappointment.

"Everybody in politics lies, but they do it with such ease, it's troubling."[1] When the Hollywood mogul David Geffen offered this stinging assessment of Bill and Hillary Clinton as the 2008 presidential campaign began, he made headlines. To some, Geffen's assessment smacked of cynicism. In fact, he was expressing an essential truth.

Politics requires artful dissembling. Those who aspire to the presidency offer large promises, while delicately skirting any complications that might call into question their ability to translate promise into reality. The Big Lies are not the pledges of tax cuts, universal health care, family values restored, or a world rendered peaceful through forceful demonstrations of American leadership. The Big Lies are the truths that remain unspoken: that freedom has an underside; that nations, like households, must ultimately live within their means; that history's purpose, the subject of so many confident pronouncements, remains inscrutable. Above all, there is this: Power is finite. Politicians pass over matters such as these in silence. As a consequence, the absence of self-awareness that forms such an enduring element of the American character persists.

At four-year intervals, ceremonies conducted to install a president reaffirm this inclination. Once again, at the anointed hour, on the steps of the Capitol, it becomes "morning in America." The slate is wiped clean. The newly inaugurated president takes office, buoyed by expectations that history will soon be restored to its proper trajectory and the nation put back on track. There is something touching about these expectations, but also something pathetic, like the battered wife who expects that this time her husband will actually keep his oft-violated vow never again to raise his hand against her.

For the abused wife, a condition of dependence condemns her to continuing torment. Salvation begins when she rejects that condition and asserts control over her life. Something of the same can be said of the American people.

For the United States the pursuit of freedom, as defined in an age of consumerism, has induced a condition of dependence—on imported goods, on imported oil, and on credit. The chief desire of the American people, whether they admit it or not, is that nothing should disrupt their access to those goods, that oil, and that credit. The chief aim of the U.S. government is to satisfy that desire, which it does in part through the distribution of largesse at home (with Congress taking a leading role) and in part through the pursuit of imperial ambitions abroad (largely the business of the executive branch).

From time to time, various public figures—even presidents—make the point that dependence may not be a good thing. Yet meaningful action to reduce this condition is notable by its absence. It's not difficult to see why. The centers of authority within Washington—above all, the White House and the upper echelons of the national security state—actually benefit from this dependency: It provides the source of status, power, and prerogatives. Imagine the impact just on the Pentagon were this country actually to achieve anything approaching energy independence. U.S. Central Command would go out of business. Dozens of bases in and around the Middle East would close. The navy's Fifth Fleet would stand down. Weapons contracts worth tens of billions would risk being canceled.

So rather than addressing the problem of dependence, members of our political class seem hell-bent on exacerbating the problem. Rather than acknowledging that American power is not limitless, they pursue policies that actually accelerate the depletion of that power. Certainly, this has been the case since 9/11.

To hard-core nationalists and neoconservatives, the acceptance of limits suggests retrenchment or irreversible decline. In fact, the reverse is true. Acknowledging the limits of American power is a precondition for stanching the losses of recent decades and for preserving the hard-won gains of earlier generations going back to the founding of the Republic. To persist in pretending that the United States is omnipotent is to exacerbate the problems that we face. The longer Americans ignore the implications of dependency and the longer policy makers nurture the pretense that this country can organize the world to its liking, the more precipitous will be its slide when the bills finally come due.

A realistic appreciation of limits, on the other hand, creates opportunities to adjust policies and replenish resources—perhaps even to renew institutions. Constraints subject old verities to reconsideration, promote fresh thinking, and unleash creativity.

Take foreign policy as an example. Reinhold Niebuhr once described the essence of statecraft as locating "the point of concurrence between the parochial and the general interest, between the national and the international common good."[2] This formulation captures the core of enlightened realism. Niebuhr understood that self-interest determines state policy. The charge to love thy neighbor applies to personal relations, not to international politics. As Niebuhr once observed, "It is not within the realm of moral possibilities to ask a nation to be 'self-sacrificing.' "[3] Yet he also understood that a nation satisfies its interests more easily when those interests are compatible with the interests of others.

During much of the Cold War, at least in its relations with key allies, the United States adhered, however imperfectly, to this concept. Under American leadership, the West achieved a solidarity that was limited and conditional, but also real and invaluable. Although breaches in allied unity occurred with some regularity, the United States and its partners patched up their disagreements (or agreed to disagree) and never allowed disputes to produce outright alienation. Many factors contributed to the remarkable durability of the Western alliance from the late 1940s through the 1980s. Prominent among them was the willingness of American statesmen to take seriously the concerns of their counterparts in countries like Germany, Japan, and the United Kingdom. Addressing the Soviet threat was an imperative, but so too was the requirement to minimize the risk of general war—here was the point of concurrence that provided the foundation of allied unity. When dealing with its partners, Washington did not simply instruct. It negotiated. In short, the United States was able to lead the West because it refrained from abusing the privileges of leadership.

After 9/11, President Bush abandoned this approach. Certain that American power had become irresistible, he showed little interest in seeking concurrence. Instead, he issued demands. No president had ever told so many other governments what they "must" do with such unvarnished insistence. Bush obliged nations to choose: They could align themselves with the United States, or they would find themselves pitted against the world's only superpower. Through his freedom agenda, the president even vowed to "rid the world of evil," with the administration claiming the prerogative of differentiating the sheep from the goats.[4]

No doubt American economic power and military power are substantial. Yet when considering the events of the past several years, above all the Iraq War, the president's "for us or against us" ultimatum appears foolhardy in the extreme, and his promise to eliminate evil, manifestly absurd. His policies have done untold damage.

Once we acknowledge that Bush's freedom agenda is unworkable and unsustainable, however, alternative approaches to strategy, informed by the Niebuhrean concept of concurrence, are not difficult to devise.

Consider, for example, the perfectly real, if far from existential threat posed by violent Islamic extremism. By overstating the Islamist danger, President Bush has committed the United States to a strategy of open-ended global war that cannot succeed. Although the Bush administration and its supporters want us to believe that alternatives to waging global war do not exist, that is nonsense.

One possible alternative is to pursue a strategy of containment. Such a strategy has worked before, against a far more formidable adversary. It can work again as a framework for erecting effective defenses. The main purpose of containment during the Cold War was to frustrate the Kremlin's efforts to extend Soviet influence. The purpose of containment today should be to prevent the sponsors of radical Islam from extending their influence.[5]

The basic orientation of this strategy is defensive; yet its ultimate aim is not to accommodate but to overcome. Cold War containment created a competition that the Soviets could not win. Over time, as the communist alternative to liberal democracy lost its appeal, the threat withered and eventually collapsed from within. A new strategy of containment should have a similar goal, allowing the inadequacies of Islamic extremism to manifest themselves and advancing the day when this threat too will wither.

Reinventing containment does not mean creating a new NATO or funding a new Marshall Plan. It does mean intensified surveillance of Islamist activity combined with sustained, multilateral police efforts to prevent terrorist attacks and to root out terrorist networks. It should also deny Islamists both the sanctuaries and the wherewithal—especially financial—needed to pursue their agenda.

Containment during the Cold War did not preclude selective engagement. Nor should it today. A strategy of containment should permit and even underwrite educational, cultural, and intellectual exchanges. It should provide opportunities for selected students from the Islamic world to study in the West. And it ought to include a public diplomacy component. Yet however worthy, such initiatives will have a marginal effect at best. Our ability to influence perceptions and attitudes across the Islamic world will remain limited.

By extension, Americans ought to give up the presumptuous notion that they are called upon to tutor Muslims in matters related to freedom and the proper relationship between politics and religion. The principle informing policy should be this: Let Islam be Islam. In the end, Muslims will have to discover for themselves the shortcomings of political Islam, much as Russians discovered the defects of Marxism-Leninism and Chinese came to appreciate the flaws of Maoism—perhaps even as we ourselves will one day begin to recognize the snares embedded in American exceptionalism.

President Bush's freedom agenda has attracted negligible international support. As a result, when it comes to liberating the Greater Middle East, the United States finds itself stuck doing most of the heavy lifting. A strategy that aims to contain violent extremists would likely be far more agreeable to American allies and could be persuaded to shoulder a greater portion of the load.

The president's insistence that war provides the best

antidote to terror has made it difficult to locate a point of concurrence between ourselves and others who share the view that Islamic extremism poses a problem, while defining the solution to that problem differently. The president's reluctance even to acknowledge the existence of other equally important problems where "the parochial and the general interest" just might intersect has further complicated the effort to forge a basis for collaboration. Repairing the legacy of the Bush years will surely require renewed attention to such problems, two of which loom especially large: nuclear weapons and climate change.

For the United States, abolishing nuclear weapons ought to be an urgent national security priority. So too should preserving our planet. These are the meta-challenges of our time. Addressing them promises to be the work of decades. Yet ridding the world of nuclear weapons is likely to prove far more plausible and achievable than ridding the world of evil. Transforming humankind's relationship to the environment, which will affect the way people live their daily lives, can hardly prove more difficult than transforming the Greater Middle East, which requires changing the way a billion or more Muslims think.

In lieu of President Bush's misguided global war on terror, these two issues offer points of concurrence that can provide the basis for sound strategy. In each case, realism rather than idealism—not "do-goodism" but self-interest—provides the impetus for action. The idea is not to save the world but to provide for the well-being of the American people. That others might credit the United States with promoting the common good, thereby refurbishing U.S. claims to global leadership, ranks at best as a secondary, although by no means trivial, potential benefit.

Nuclear weapons are unusable. Their employment in any conceivable scenario would be a political and moral catastrophe. For the United States, they are becoming unnecessary, even as a deterrent. Certainly, they are unlikely to dissuade the adversaries most likely to employ such weapons against us—Islamic extremists intent on acquiring their own nuclear capability.

If anything, the opposite is true. By retaining a strategic arsenal in readiness (and by insisting without qualification that the dropping of atomic bombs on two Japanese cities in 1945 was justified), the United States continues tacitly to sustain the view that nuclear weapons play a legitimate role in international politics—this at a time when our own interests are best served by doing everything possible to reinforce the existing taboo against their further use.

Furthermore, the day is approaching when the United States will be able to deter other nuclear-armed states, like Russia and China, without itself relying on nuclear weapons. Modern conventional weapons possess the potential to provide a more effective foundation for deterrence. They offer highly lethal, accurate, responsive second-strike (or even first-strike) capabilities. Precision conventional weapons also carry fewer of the moral complications that make nuclear weapons so inherently problematic. Hence, they have the added advantage of being usable, which enhances credibility.

By the end of the Cold War, the United States had accumulated a stockpile of some 23,000 nuclear weapons. By 2007, that number stood at an estimated 5,736 warheads of various types.[6] Although the reduction appears impressive, this represents less an achievement than a gesture—like the chronic cigarette smoker who goes from three packs a day to two and fancies that he has his habit under control. Even if one assumes that nuclear weapons possess any real utility, what conceivable target set would require more than 100 warheads to destroy? Far more severe cuts in the U.S. arsenal, shrinking the total to a couple hundred at most, are in order.

When it comes to nuclear weapons, the point of concurrence between the parochial and the general interest seems clear: Such weapons should be entirely eliminated. Presidents from Harry Truman's day to the present have bemoaned their very existence and have repeatedly promised to work for their abolition. Now might actually be the moment to act on that promise.

Climate change likewise poses a looming threat to America's well-being—and the world's. Here, the point of concurrence between the national and international common good seems self-evident: It lies in moving aggressively to reduce the level of emissions that contribute to global warming.

The United States ranks among the world's worst polluters—here we confront one unfortunate by-product of American freedom as currently practiced. Acting alone, Americans cannot curb climate change. Yet unless the United States acts, the chances of effectively addressing this global threat are nil.

Preserving the environment means reducing the global consumption of fossil fuels while developing alternative energy sources. In addition to saving the planet, leadership in this arena will enhance national security. Among other things, reducing oil imports could reduce the flow of dollars to the Islamists who wish us ill, something that ought to be the very cornerstone of a strategy of containment. Perfect security is an illusion. Yet when it comes to keeping security problems within tolerable limits, self-sufficiency has a value greater than even the largest army.

No doubt undertaking a serious, long-term, national effort to begin the transition to a post–fossil fuel economy promises to be a costly proposition. Yet whereas spending trillions to forcibly democratize the Islamic world will achieve little, investing trillions in energy research might actually produce something useful. From the Manhattan Project to the space race to the development of the Internet, large-scale technological innovation has tended to be an American strong suit. By comparison, when it comes to large-scale efforts to engineer political, social, and cultural change abroad, the American track record has never been better than mixed. Since September 2001, it has been downright abysmal.

A concerted effort to abolish nuclear weapons will entail some risk. A concerted effort to reduce the effects of climate change implies considerable inconvenience and even sacrifice, at least in the near term. Yet a people for whom freedom has become synonymous with consumption and self-actualization evince little appetite for either risk or sacrifice—even if inaction today increases the prospect of greater risks and more painful sacrifices tomorrow.

As long as Americans remain in denial—insisting that the power of the United States is without limits—they will remain unlikely to do any of these things. Instead, abetted by their political leaders, they will continue to fancy that some version of global war offers an antidote to Islamic radicalism. The United States will modernize and enhance its nuclear strike capabilities while professing outrage that others should seek similar capabilities. Americans will treat climate change as a problem to be nickel-and-dimed. They will guzzle imported oil, binge on imported goods, and indulge in imperial dreams. All the while, Washington will issue high-minded proclamations testifying to the approaching triumph of democracy everywhere and forever.

Meanwhile, the American people will ignore the imperative of settling accounts—balancing budgets, curbing consumption, and paying down debt. They will remain passive as politicians fritter away U.S. military might on unnecessary wars. They will permit officials responsible for failed policies to dodge accountability. They will tolerate stupefy-ing incompetence and dysfunction in the nation's capital, counting on the next president to fix everything that the last one screwed up. In Niebuhr's words, they will cling to "a culture which makes 'living standards' the final norm of the good life and which regards the perfection of techniques as the guarantor of every cultural as well as every social-moral value."[7] Above all, they will venerate freedom while carefully refraining from assessing its content or measuring its costs.

"The trustful acceptance of false solutions for our per-plexing problems," Niebuhr wrote a half century ago, "adds a touch of pathos to the tragedy of our age."[8] That judgment remains valid today. Adamantly insisting that it is unique among history's great powers, the United States seems likely to follow the well-worn path taken by others, blind to the perils that it courts through its own feckless behavior.

For all nations, Niebuhr once observed, "The desire to gain an immediate selfish advantage always imperils their ultimate interests. If they recognize this fact, they usually recognize it too late."[9] Both parts of this dictum apply to the United States today—and in spades. To extend however slightly the here and now, Americans are increasingly in-clined to write off the future. So they carry on, heedless of the consequences even for themselves, no less for their chil-dren or grandchildren.

Thus does the tragedy of our age move inexorably to-ward its conclusion. "To the end of history," our prophet once wrote, "social orders will probably destroy themselves in the effort to prove that they are indestructible."[10] Cling-ing doggedly to the conviction that the rules to which other nations must submit don't apply, Americans appear deter-mined to affirm Niebuhr's axiom of willful self-destruction.

Afterword

This book, with its core message emphasizing "the imperative of putting America's house in order," first appeared in bookstores in mid-August 2008. Its introduction contained this warning: "The day of reckoning approaches."

Within a matter of weeks, that day arrived, in the form of the gravest economic crisis to confront the United States since the Great Depression. On Wall Street, stock prices collapsed. Venerable banking firms vanished. Retirement savings plans sustained losses in the trillions. Hundreds of thousands of workers lost their jobs—over a million in the last two months of 2008 alone. Corporate executives trooped to Washington, tin cups extended, petitioning Congress for handouts. References to "frozen markets," "credit crunch," "toxic assets," and "securitized derivatives" filled the airways, enriching the American vernacular.

In hopes of pulling the economy out of its tailspin, the

outgoing administration of George W. Bush embarked upon a massive spending spree. This so-called stimulus package failed. Undaunted by that failure or by the prospect of inheriting a projected trillion-dollar budget deficit, then–president-elect Barack Obama vowed to redouble stimulus efforts. It was going to be 1933 all over again: the New Deal 2.0. To get workers working and consumers consuming, the incoming administration promised to spend up to $850 billion over two years. Where was this money going to come from? Few even bothered to ask.

Fewer still drew any correlation between economic distress at home and the predicament into which the United States had worked itself abroad. As far as Washington was concerned (either George W. Bush's or Barack Obama's), domestic and foreign policies continued to occupy two different, largely unrelated spheres. Nothing that had occurred during the eight years of the second Bush era, it seemed, had overturned that conviction.

That President Bush should persist in such a view was hardly surprising. By the time he left office, his administration's list of notable accomplishments had shrunk to a single item: the prevention of a literal recurrence of 9/11. By waging wars in Iraq and Afghanistan, he had kept Americans "safe"—so, at least, the president's most devoted acolytes vigorously insisted. To admit to a possible causal relationship between the economic calamity of 2008 and the untold billions expended pursuant to Bush's global war on terror would necessarily rob this last remaining claim of its luster.

If President Obama remains similarly oblivious to any correlation between the nation's economic woes and the flawed national security policies he inherited, that will be far more puzzling, however. After all, the moment you acknowledge the linkage between Bush's ill-advised global war and our current economic disarray, whole new avenues of analysis open up. Getting to root causes suddenly becomes a possibility. It's akin to recognizing that smoking causes cancer or that prolonged alcohol abuse can produce liver damage: to make the connection is to redefine the problem. New strategies of prevention present themselves. The chief one: avoid patently self-destructive behavior.

No single factor can explain the extraordinary excitement generated by Barack Obama's successful run for the White House. The candidate's intelligence, vigor, eloquence, cool persona, and compelling personal story all figured in important ways. Self-discipline, impressive organizational skills, and a pronounced knack for raising money certainly helped. Yet the key to Obama's victory lay in his oft-repeated promise to "change the way Washington works." Obama's very election expressed a popular desire, as deep-seated as it was widespread, to repudiate all that Washington had come to represent in the era of George W. Bush.

Satisfying this yearning for change, however, implies something more than tacking from starboard to port. On November 4, 2008, the millions who watched Obama claim his victory in Chicago's Grant Park—"Because of what we did, on this day change has come to America"—were counting on the nation's new captain to set the United States on an entirely different azimuth, headed toward a new and better destination.

Yet substantive change will remain little more than a slogan absent a willingness to consider this proposition: When it comes to national security, the standard navigational charts used to guide the ship of state are obsolete. The assumptions, doctrines, habits, and routines falling under the rubric of "national security policy" have outlived their usefulness. The antidote to the disappointments and failures of the Bush years, illustrated most vividly in the never-ending wars in Iraq and Afghanistan, is not to try harder, but to think differently. Only then will it become possible to avoid the patently self-destructive behavior that today finds Americans facing the prospect of perpetual conflict that neither our army nor our economy can sustain.

That President Obama will find a way out of this predicament—that he will make good on his promise of change—must be the fervent hope of all persons of good will. Doing so will require not only ideas but the people and the wherewithal to implement those ideas.

To fill his cabinet and to staff the White House, Obama has recruited an impressive array of talent. Yet whether his chief lieutenants will serve as agents of real change—or whether they will settle, as is so often the case in Washington, for some modest updating—remains to be seen.

Consider Obama's national security team, headed by Secretary of State Hillary Clinton, Secretary of Defense Robert Gates, General James Jones as national security adviser, and Admiral Dennis Blair as director of national intelligence. Each and every one is a seasoned professional: competent, well-informed, pragmatic, and wise in the ways of Washington. Yet however imposing their résumés, they are establishment figures, utterly conventional in their outlook. That a career intelligence official like Gates or a retired Marine four-star like Jones will question the core assumptions informing standard national security practices is by no means an impossibility. It's just not especially likely. One might as well look to the CEOs of Detroit's Big Three to promote mass transit as a preferred alternative to the automobile.

Even before Obama's inauguration, observers alert to the slightest hint of backsliding complained that the incoming national security team seemed less likely to challenge the status quo than to preserve it. Obama was quick to deflect this charge: He himself would function as the engine of transformation. "Understand where the vision for change comes from, first and foremost," he explained. "It comes from me. That's my job. . . ."

This is a large responsibility for any single individual to take on. Given Obama's sparse national security credentials, the challenge he has set for himself is nothing short of daunting.

On the campaign trail, when addressing matters of national security, Obama offered views that were not so much novel as carefully constructed. On the one hand, he denounced all the worst excesses of the Bush era. Ending the Iraq War, closing Guantanamo, and prohibiting any further resort to "enhanced interrogation techniques": these became signature themes of his candidacy. Yet Obama also spoke of leaving a sizable "residual" force in Iraq, promised to send more U.S. troops to Afghanistan, and hinted at a willingness to expand U.S. military operations in Pakistan, even if that meant disregarding Pakistani claims of sovereignty.

Prior to November 4th, Obama's hawkish posturing on these issues may have reflected a conscious effort to insulate himself from charges, regularly flung at Democrats, of being soft on national security. At least implicitly, however, he also appeared to signal his own personal commitment to the global war on terror, a term he continued to use. Candidate Obama differed with Bush (and with the man who ran against him, Senator John McCain) not on fundamental principles but on operational priorities. Obama never directly questioned the wisdom of perpetuating the global war that Bush had conceived; he merely conveyed the sense that he would fight that war more effectively.

Should President Obama's actions in office affirm open-ended armed conflict as his preferred antidote to violent

Islamic radicalism, Bush himself and his dwindling band of supporters will no doubt rejoice. In that event, however, Obama will run the risk of seeing his presidency hijacked. Just as, forty years ago, Richard Nixon quickly discovered that Lyndon Johnson's war became his, so too Obama will face the prospect of Bush's wars, especially in Afghanistan, becoming his own. And the likelihood of his making good on his promise of change will diminish accordingly.

In Grant Park on November 4, Obama declared that the time had come for Americans "to put their hands on the arc of history and bend it once more toward the hope of a better day." That our history has a discernible arc and that Americans possess the capacity to bend it to their will are propositions to which any number of earlier presidents—Obama's immediate predecessor not least among them—have fervently subscribed.

Perhaps this solemn genuflection before the altar of American exceptionalism amounted to little more than a rhetorical flourish meant to punctuate a night of exuberant celebration. We must hope so. This much we can say with certainty: If Obama's vision of change really does center on the expectation of somehow taming history, then he and his supporters are headed for disappointment.

More than half a century ago, Reinhold Niebuhr warned Americans against what he called "our dreams of managing history." As someone who professes to admire the great Protestant theologian, President Obama should heed Niebuhr's warning.

Were he alive today, Niebuhr would likely call upon Obama to reject the cant and clichés that have for too long substituted for serious political discourse. He would urge the president not to succumb, as Bush did, to an illusory and misleading version of the American past. He would in-

sist upon the imperative of seeing the world as it is and ourselves as we really are—as, I hope, this book does. He would
invite Obama to consider this possibility: The principal explanation for the fix in which the country finds itself today
lies in our own folly.

President Bush interpreted 9/11 as a summons: To preserve the American way of life, he set out to transform the
Islamic world. This proved to be a costly misjudgment, producing few benefits for the American people despite the expenditure of vast quantities of blood and treasure. Bush's
record merits sober reflection: It offers a foretaste of the consequences awaiting a nation that persists in exempting itself
from the rules to which all others must conform.

The truth is this: A world that once indulged American
profligacy is no longer willing to do so. Nor does the United
States possess reserves of hard power sufficient to oblige the
world to accommodate itself to our desires. We don't have
the money and we don't have the troops; of the many lessons to be drawn from the Bush era, this stands out as the
most important. To preserve that which we value most in the
American way of life, therefore, requires modifying that way
of life, discriminating between things that are essential and
those that are not.

If Obama grasps this essential point and acts on it, he
just might fulfill the expectations of those to whom he is
such a symbol of hope. If, however, he indulges the pretense
that our way of life is sacrosanct and our power without limits, then hope will surely give way to disillusionment.

Boston, Massachusetts
January 25, 2009

Notes

Introduction: War Without Exits

1. John Lewis Gaddis, *The Long Peace: Inquiries into the History of the Cold War* (New York, 1989).
2. As a description of the post-9/11 conflict, the phrase is attributed to General John Abizaid, commander of U.S. Central Command from 2003 to 2007. Bradley Graham and Josh White, "Abizaid Credited with Popularizing the Term 'Long War,'" *Washington Post*, February 3, 2006.
3. Those who did question the assumption of permanent American supremacy tended to be foreigners, which makes them easier to ignore. See, for example, Emmanuel Todd, *After the Empire: The Breakdown of the American Order* (New York, 2002).
4. Bill Gertz, "General Foresees 'Generational War' against Terrorism," *Washington Times*, December 13, 2006.
5. Donald Rumsfeld, "A New Kind of War," *New York Times*, September 27, 2001.
6. Reinhold Niebuhr, *The Irony of American History* (New York, 1952), p. 91.
7. Ibid., p. 3.

8. D. B. Robertson, *Love and Justice: Selections from the Shorter Writings of Reinhold Niebuhr* (Cleveland, Ohio, 1957), p. 97.

9. Reinhold Niebuhr, *The World Crisis and American Responsibility* (New York, 1958), p. 125.

10. Quoted in Ron Suskind, *The Price of Loyalty: George W. Bush, the White House, and the Education of Paul O'Neill* (New York, 2004), p. 291.

11. Robert Kagan, "Power and Weakness," *Policy Review*, June–July 2002.

12. Reinhold Niebuhr, *Beyond Tragedy* (New York, 1937), p. 39.

1. The Crisis of Profligacy

1. A classic example, dated but still important, is Christopher Lasch, *The Culture of Narcissism* (New York, 1978).

2. Alexis de Tocqueville, *Democracy in America* (New Rochelle, N.Y., 1965 [orig. 1835]), part 2, chap. 13.

3. Woodrow Wilson, "Campaign Address," Jersey City, N.J., May 25, 1912.

4. Frederick Jackson Turner, *The Frontier in American History* (New York, 1921), chap. 11.

5. David M. Potter, *People of Plenty* (Chicago, 1954), p. 126.

6. William A. Williams, *Empire as a Way of Life* (New York, 1980), p. ix.

7. Niebuhr, *Irony of American History*, pp. 59–60.

8. Paul Kennedy, *The Rise and Fall of the Great Powers* (New York, 1987), p. 358.

9. Thomas G. Paterson and J. Garry Clifford, *America Ascendant* (Lexington, Mass., 1995), p. 87.

10. U.S. Department of Commerce, *Statistical Abstract of the United States, 1950*, table 998, p. 839.

11. Kennedy, *Rise and Fall*, p. 358.

12. Williamson Murray and Alan R. Millett, *A War to Be Won* (Cambridge, Mass., 2000), p. 564.

13. As Michael C. C. Adams writes, "The gap between the top fifth and the bottom fifth in income actually narrowed for the only time in the century." Adams, *The Best War Ever* (Baltimore, Md., 1994), pp. 114, 131.

14. Charles S. Maier, *Among Empires: American Ascendancy and Its Predecessors* (Cambridge, Mass., 2006), chap. 5.

15. Ibid., p. 225.

16. U.S. Department of Commerce, *Statistical Abstract of the United States, 2007*, table 895.
17. WTRG Economics, "Oil Price History and Analysis," http://www.wtrg.com/prices.htm, accessed July 13, 2007.
18. U.S. Department of Commerce, *Statistical Abstract of the United States, 2007*, table 1283.
19. Francis X. Clines, "About Chautauqua," *New York Times*, August 2, 1979.
20. Eugene Kennedy, "Carter Agonistes," *New York Times Magazine*, August 5, 1979.
21. Congressional Budget Office, "Revenues, Outlays, Surpluses, Deficits, and Debt Held by the Public, 1962–2006," http://www.cbo.gov/budget/historical.pdf, accessed July 20, 2007.
22. U.S. Department of Commerce, *Statistical Abstract of the United States, 2007*, table 280.
23. Reinhold Niebuhr, *Moral Man and Immoral Society* (New York, 1932), p. 95.
24. U.S. Department of Commerce, Bureau of Economic Analysis, "International Investment Position of the United States at Yearend, 1976–2006," http://www.bea.gov/international/index.htm, accessed July 21, 2007.
25. Federal Reserve Bank of St. Louis, "Personal Saving Rate," http://research.stlouisfed.org/fred2/data/PSAVERT.txt, accessed July 21, 2007.
26. Michael Calabrese and Maya MacGuineas, "Spendthrift Nation," *Atlantic*, January–February 2003, pp. 102–6.
27. National Commission on Terrorist Attacks Upon the United States, *The 9/11 Commission Report* (Washington, D.C., 2004), sec. 2.3, p. 55.
28. Ronald Reagan, "Proclamation 4908—Afghanistan Day," March 10, 1982, http://www.reagan.utexas.edu/archives/speeches/1982/31082c.htm, accessed July 27, 2007.
29. Olga Oliker and David A. Shlapak, *U.S. Interests in Central Asia: Policy Priorities and Military Roles* (Santa Monica, Calif., 2005), p. v. This monograph was prepared by the RAND Corporation for the U.S. Air Force.
30. Beth Jones, assistant secretary of state for European and Eurasian affairs, "U.S. Relations with Central Asia," February 11, 2002, http://www.state.gov/p/eur/rls/rm/2002/7946.htm, accessed July 31, 2007.

31. Niebuhr, *Irony of American History*, p. 78.

32. Marc J. O'Reilly, *Unexceptional: America's Empire in the Persian Gulf, 1941–2007* (Lanham, Md., 2008), p. 154.

33. U.S. Department of Commerce, *Statistical Abstract of the United States, 2007*, table 905.

34. Ibid., table 1283.

35. Ibid., table 459.

36. Robert Kagan, "Saddam's Impending Victory," *Weekly Standard*, February 2, 1998.

37. Donald Rumsfeld, "Address to the Men and Women of Whiteman Air Force Base," October 19, 2001.

38. A handful of second-tier politicians expressed doubts about the direction of U.S. policy after 9/11, with Senator Robert Byrd (Democrat, West Virginia) offering a prime example. Byrd wielded little influence, however, and his dissent went all but unnoticed. Still, his was a position of honor.

39. Bill Keller, "The Sunshine Warrior," *New York Times Magazine*, September 22, 2002.

40. Mark Danner, "The Struggles of Democracy and Empire," *New York Times*, October 9, 2002.

41. Franklin D. Roosevelt, "State of the Union Address," January 6, 1942.

42. Institute for the Analysis of Global Security, "Energy Security," http://www.iags.org/energysecurity.html, accessed July 16, 2007.

43. U.S. Department of Commerce, Bureau of Economic Analysis, "National Economic Accounts: Personal Savings Rate," http://www.bea.gov/briefrm/saving.htm, accessed July 16, 2007.

44. U.S. Census Bureau, "Annual Trade Highlights, 2006," http://www.census.gov/foreign-trade/statistics/highlights/annual.html#notes, accessed July 16, 2007.

45. "The Debt to the Penny and Who Holds It," www.TreasuryDirect.gov/NP/BPDlogin?application-np, accessed July 16, 2007.

46. Barry Schwartz, Hazel Rose Markus, and Alana Conner Snibbe, "Is Freedom Just Another Word for Many Things to Buy?" *New York Times Magazine*, February 26, 2006.

47. Max Boot, "Uncle Sam Wants Tu," *Los Angeles Times*, February 24, 2005.

48. Tom Regan, "Report: Iraq War Costs Could Top $2 Trillion," *Christian Science Monitor*, January 10, 2006.

49. The Concord Coalition, "Relevant Numbers on Federal Debt," July 6, 2006, http://www.concordcoalition.org/issues/feddebt/debt-facts.html, accessed August 7, 2007.

50. A representative example is Peter G. Peterson, *Running on Empty: How the Democratic and Republican Parties Are Bankrupting Our Future and What Americans Can Do About It* (New York, 2004). For a colorful rendering of the same argument, see James Fallows, "Countdown to a Meltdown," *Atlantic,* July–August 2005, pp. 51–64.

2. The Political Crisis

1. Reinhold Niebuhr, *The Children of Light and the Children of Darkness* (New York, 1944), p. xiv.

2. In a broader sense, the practice of citing national emergencies as a rationale for enhancing executive power began in earnest on March 6, 1933. On that date, two days after becoming president, Franklin D. Roosevelt issued a proclamation declaring a state of national emergency and ordering a bank holiday, thereby inaugurating the New Deal. The U.S. government has operated in a condition defined by emergency ever since.

3. Quoted in Jack Goldsmith, *The Terror Presidency* (New York, 2007), p. 126.

4. In the House, 391 incumbents ran for reelection and all but 22 of them won. In the Senate, 27 of 33 incumbents running for reelection won.

5. "Pelosi Statement on the Fourth Anniversary of the Iraq War," March 16, 2007, http://www.house.gov/pelosi/press/releases/March07/Iraq.html, accessed October 9, 2007.

6. Dean Acheson, *Present at the Creation* (New York, 1969), p. 376.

7. Bill Clinton, "A New Covenant for America," Georgetown University, December 12, 1991.

8. Barack Obama, "Renewing American Leadership," *Foreign Affairs,* July–August 2007.

9. Niebuhr, *Beyond Tragedy,* pp. 145–46.

10. C. Wright Mills, *The Power Elite* (New York, 1956, rpt. 2000).

11. Ibid., p. 222.

12. James Chace and Caleb Carr, *America Invulnerable* (New York, 1988), p. 13.

13. Quoted in Ron Suskind, *The One Percent Doctrine* (New York, 2006), p. 62.

14. "Pentagon Facts and Figures," http://pentagon.afis.osd.mil/facts.cfm, accessed December 6, 2007.

15. Lewis Mumford, *The City in History* (New York, 1961), p. 433.

16. U.S. Supreme Court, *United States v. Reynolds, 345 U.S. 1* (1953), http://caselaw.lp.findlaw.com/scripts/getcase.pl?navby=CASE&court=US&vol=345&page=1, accessed September 16, 2007.

17. Barry Siegel, "State-Secret Overreach," *Los Angeles Times*, September 16, 2007.

18. Paul Yingling, "A Failure in Generalship," *Armed Forces Journal*, May 2007.

19. "Rice: 'Slam Dunk' Comment Didn't Lead to War," *CNN.com* (April 29, 2007), http://www.cnn.com/2007/POLITICS/04/29/rice.tenet/index.html?iref–ewssearch, accessed September 25, 2007.

20. Eisenhower personally chaired 329 of the 366 NSC meetings during his eight years as president. Fred Greenstein and Richard H. Immerman, "Effective National Security Advising: Recovering the Eisenhower Legacy," *Political Science Quarterly* 115 (Autumn 2000): 341.

21. Andrew J. Bacevich, "The Paradox of Professionalism: Eisenhower, Ridgway, and the Challenge to Civilian Control, 1953–1955," *Journal of Military History* 61 (April 1997): 303–34; David Alan Rosenberg, "The Origins of Overkill: Nuclear Weapons and American Strategy, 1946–1960," *International Security* 7 (Spring 1983): 3–71.

22. Tim Weiner, *Legacy of Ashes: The History of the CIA* (New York, 2007), pp. 71–167. Eisenhower described his efforts to establish an effective intelligence community responsive to his will as "an eight-year defeat." Weiner, p. 167.

23. Completed in 1962, the inspector general's report was finally declassified in February 1998. It appeared in published form as Peter Kornbluh, ed., *Bay of Pigs Declassified: The Secret CIA Report on the Invasion of Cuba* (New York, 1998).

24. Richard Reeves, *President Kennedy: Profile of Power* (New York, 1993), pp. 97, 103.

25. Ernest R. May and Philip D. Zelikow, eds., *The Kennedy Tapes: Inside the White House During the Cuban Missile Crisis* (Cambridge, Mass., 1997), p. 28.

26. Maxwell D. Taylor, *Swords and Plowshares* (New York, 1972), p. 252.

27. Bob Woodward, *Plan of Attack* (New York, 2004), pp. 1–8.

28. A recent example: A project called "Beyond Goldwater-Nichols," sponsored by the Center for Strategic and International Studies in Washington, proposes new reforms aimed at imparting to the national security bureaucracy the "coherence and agility" required for an "age of continuous threat." *Beyond Goldwater-Nichols: U.S. Government and Defense Reform for a New Strategic Era* (Washington, D.C., 2005), p. 13.

29. *Reorganization of the Department of Defense: Hearings Before the Armed Services Committee, United States Senate,* 99th Congress, First Session (Washington, D.C., 1987), p. 28.

30. Quoted in Charles A. Stevenson, *Warriors and Politicians: U.S. Civil-Military Relations Under Stress* (New York, 2006), p. 183.

31. Quoted in Michael H. Hunt, *The American Ascendancy: How the United States Gained and Wielded Global Dominance* (Chapel Hill, N.C., 2007), p. 149.

32. Acheson, *Present at the Creation,* p. 375.

33. The quotation reflects the summary judgment of Stimson's official biographer. Elting E. Morison, *Turmoil and Tradition: A Study of the Life and Times of Henry L. Stimson* (Boston, 1960), p. 654.

34. For an excellent biography, see Townsend Hoopes and Douglas Brinkley, *Driven Patriot: The Life and Times of James Forrestal* (New York, 1992).

35. Ibid., pp. 262, 265.

36. All quotations come from the original text which is available at "NSC 68: United States Programs and Objective for National Security," April 14, 1950, http://www.fas.org/irp/offdocs/nsc-hst/nsc-68.htm, accessed October 22, 2007.

37. Max Boot, "What Next? The Foreign Policy Agenda Beyond Iraq," *Weekly Standard,* May 5, 2003; Thomas Donnelly, "The Underpinnings of the Bush Doctrine," *AEI National Security Outlook,* January 31, 2003; Frederick W. Kagan, "The Korean Parallel: Is It June 1950 All Over Again?" *Weekly Standard,* October 8, 2001. The quote is from Kagan.

38. Frederick W. Kagan, "Back to the Future: NSC-68 and the Right Course for America Today," *SAIS Review* 19 (1999): 55.

39. Robin Wright, "From the Desk of Donald Rumsfeld . . . ," *Washington Post,* November 1, 2007.

40. An ironic illustration of this practice is found in the Nixon Center for Peace and Freedom, a Washington think tank named in honor of the disgraced thirty-seventh president. Nixon himself continually referred to *peace* and *freedom* as abiding objectives of U.S. foreign policy and his own fondest hopes for the world. Yet with the possible exception of Henry Kissinger, no one was more practiced than Nixon in infusing such terms with meanings at odds with their commonplace definitions.

41. "The Secret Downing Street Memo," *Sunday Times* (London), May 1, 2005.

42. Paul Wolfowitz, "Statesmanship in the New Century," in Robert Kagan and William Kristol, eds., *Present Dangers: Crisis and Opportunity in American Foreign and Defense Policy* (San Francisco, Calif., 2000), p. 314.

43. Ibid., p. 334.

44. "Deputy Secretary Wolfowitz Interview with Sam Tannenhaus, Vanity Fair," May 9, 2003, http://www.defenselink.mil/transcripts/transcript.aspx?transcriptid=2594, accessed December 6, 2007.

45. Paul Wolfowitz, "Iraq: What Does Disarmament Look Like?" presentation made to the Council on Foreign Relations, New York, January 23, 2003, http://www.cfr.org/publication.html?id=5454, accessed December 5, 2007.

46. Paul Wolfowitz, "United on the Risks of a War with Iraq," *Washington Post,* December 23, 2002.

47. Niebuhr, *Beyond Tragedy,* p. 98.

48. Zalmay M. Khalilzad and Paul Wolfowitz, "Overthrow Him," *Weekly Standard,* December 1, 1997.

49. Quoted in Ron Suskind, "Faith, Certainty, and the Presidency of George W. Bush," *New York Times Magazine,* October 17, 2004.

50. Niebuhr, *Irony of American History,* p. 88.

51. Wolfowitz, "Statesmanship in the New Century," p. 335.

3. The Military Crisis

1. Corelli Barnett, *The Swordbearers* (New York, 1964), p. 11.

2. "President Bush Delivers Graduation Speech at West Point," June 1, 2002, http://www.whitehouse.gov/news/releases/2002/06/20020601-3.html, accessed November 19, 2007.

3. David Frum and Richard Perle, *An End to Evil* (New York, 2003), p. 33.

4. Tommy Franks, *American Soldier* (New York, 2004), p. 546.

5. Max Boot, "Doctrine of the Big Enchilada," *Washington Post,* October 14, 2002.

6. Max Boot, "The New American Way of War," *Foreign Affairs,* July–August 2003.

7. "President Bush Outlines Progress in Operation Iraqi Freedom," St. Louis, Mo., April 16, 2004, http://www.whitehouse.gov/news/releases/2003/04/20030416-9.html, accessed December 10, 2007.

8. *Joint Vision 2010,* http://www.dtic.mil/jv2010/jv2010.pdf, accessed November 21, 2007; General Henry H. Shelton, "Visualizing Joint Vision 2010," *Air Force Journal,* Fall 1998.

9. Colin Powell, *My American Journey* (New York, 1995), p. 532.

10. Ibid., p. 576.

11. Robert Kaplan, *Imperial Grunts* (New York, 2005), pp. 3, 31.

12. Michael Barone, "Surge 101," *National Review Online,* December 29, 2007.

13. For a senior military officer's description of this future, see Lieutenant General Peter Chiarelli, "Learning from Our Modern Wars," *Military Review,* September–October 2007.

14. Robert M. Gates, "Remarks to the Association of the United States Army," October 10, 2007, http://www.defenselink.mil/speeches/speech.aspx?speechid=1181, accessed December 24, 2007.

15. The content of U.S. Army Field Manual 3-24 *Counterinsurgency* and the publicity accompanying its appearance in 2006 both testify to the extent to which this first lesson of the Iraq War has captured the attention not only of the officer corps but also of the informed public. In 2007, the University of Chicago Press published verbatim its own edition of FM 3-24, marketing the field manual as a textbook.

16. "Republican General: Rummy Responsible for Deaths, Failure, Abu Ghraib . . . ," September 25, 2006, http://alternet.org/blogs/video/42137/, accessed December 23, 2007.

17. Adrian R. Lewis, *The American Culture of War* (New York, 2007), p. 377. Emphasis in the original.

18. David Corn, "McCain in NH: Would Be 'Fine' to Keep Troops in Iraq for 'a Hundred Years,'" *MoJo Blog,* January 3, 2008, www

.motherjones.com/mojoblog/archives/2008/01/6735_mccain_in
_nh_wo.html, accessed January 24, 2008.

19. The U.S. Army Command and Staff College has republished
Trinquier. See http://www-cgsc.army.mil/carl/resources/csi/
trinquier/trinquier.asp. The Air War College has made the Small
Wars Manual available on the Internet at http://www.au.af.mil/
au/awc/awcgate/swm/index.htm. In 2006, Praeger issued a new
edition of Galula's book.

20. Perhaps more precisely, once the United States had acquired
Puerto Rico, the Panama Canal Zone, and the Virgin Islands, it
had no interest in additional Caribbean colonies.

21. See, for example, Clark's account of the Kosovo War, *Waging Modern War* (New York, 2001).

22. "Secretary Rumsfeld Interview with Barry Schweid, Associated
Press," August 3, 2004, http://www.defenselink.mil/transcripts/
transcript.aspx?transcriptid=2490, accessed January 24, 2008.

23. Quoted in Woodward, *Plan of Attack*, p. 281. In a memoir published later that year, Franks chose a slightly different formulation, describing Feith as "the dumbest fucking guy on the
planet." See Franks, *American Soldier*, p. 362.

24. "President Presents Medal of Freedom," December 14, 2004,
http://www.whitehouse.gov/news/releases/2004/12/20041214-3
.html, accessed December 26, 2007.

25. Franks, *American Soldier*, pp. 276–77, 373, 545.

26. Ibid., p. 313.

27. Ibid., p. 295.

28. Ibid., pp. 338, 377.

29. Michael R. Gordon and Bernard E. Trainor, *The Generals' War* (Boston, 1995), pp. 443–50.

30. The charge against Aspin was that he had denied General Montgomery's request for reinforcements: AC-130 gunships and M1
Abrams tanks. Yet in subsequently testimony, General Garrison,
commander of the rangers who became embroiled in the Mogadishu firefight, said explicitly that neither the additional firepower nor the armored vehicles would have changed the outcome.
"It is highly debatable that the AC-130s would have made a difference," he told the Senate Armed Services Committee. "As for its
shooting capabilities, i.e., pouring lead on the target, I don't know

how much more lead could have been applied." With regard to the Abrams tanks, Garrison testified, "I never considered it useful to integrate armor into a raid." He continued: "If I had tanks, I don't know if I would have used them. I never thought of a contingency plan for backups of equipment like tanks and APCs [armored personnel carriers]." Senator John Warner and Senator Carl Levin, "Review of the Circumstances Surrounding the Ranger Raid on October 3–4, 1993, in Mogadishu, Somalia," September 29, 1995, pp. 30, 33. This document, commonly referred to as the Warner-Levin Report, provides the results of a Senate Armed Services Committee investigation of the incident.

31. Clark, *Waging Modern War*, p. 86.

32. Ibid., p. 119.

33. William M. Arkin, "Operation Allied Force: 'The Most Precise Application of Air Power in History,'" in Andrew J. Bacevich and Eliot A. Cohen, eds., *War Over Kosovo* (New York, 2001), pp. 21–22.

34. Winston S. Churchill, *The World Crisis, 1911–1918* (London, 1931), p. 298.

35. Congressional Budget Office, "Estimated Cost of the Administration's Proposal to Increase the Army's and the Marine Corps's Personnel Levels," April 16, 2007, p. 2.

36. "DoD News Briefing—Secretary Rumsfeld—and Gen. Myers," January 7, 2003, http://www.globalsecurity.org/military/library/news/2003/01/mil-030107-dod02.htm, accessed December 29, 2007.

37. Carl von Clausewitz, *On War* (Princeton, N.J., 1976), book 1, chap. 3, p. 101.

38. Winston Churchill, *My Early Life* (New York, rpt. 1996), p. 232.

39. Quoted in Greg Jaffe, "Rumsfeld's Vindication Promises a Change in Tactics, Deployment," *Wall Street Journal*, April 10, 2003.

40. Ibid.

41. Barbara Slavin and Dave Moniz, "War in Iraq's Aftermath Hits Troops Hard," *USA Today*, July 21, 2003.

42. Evan Thomas and John Barry, "A New Way of War," *Newsweek*, August 20, 2007.

43. Clay Wilson, "Improvised Explosive Devices in Iraq and Afghanistan: Effects and Countermeasures," CRS Report for Congress, Congressional Research Service, August 28, 2007, p. 6.

44. By the end of 2007, IEDs had caused approximately 40 percent of

all U.S. military fatalities in Iraq. Brookings Institution, "Iraq Index," November 29, 2007, http://www.brookings.edu/saban/~/media/Files/Centers/Saban/Iraq%20Index/index20071129.pdf, accessed January 2, 2008.

45. Eli Lake, "Electricity Minister: Baghdad Power at Pre-War Level by 2011," *New York Sun*, December 10, 2007.

46. October 2007 quarterly report of the Special Inspector General for Iraq Reconstruction, pp. 115, 121.

47. Government Accountability Office, *DoD Cannot Ensure That U.S.-Funded Equipment Has Reached Iraqi Security Forces*, July 2007.

48. Colum Lynch and Griff Witte, "Afghan Opium Trade Hits New Peak," *Washington Post*, August 28, 2007.

49. Norman Mailer, *The Naked and the Dead* (New York, 1948), p. 578. The citation is to the Modern Library Edition.

50. Ron Suskind, *The One Percent Doctrine* (New York, 2006).

51. "President Bush Delivers Graduation Speech at West Point," June 1, 2002, http://www.whitehouse.gov/news/releases/2002/06/20020601-3.html, accessed January 1, 2008.

52. Niebuhr, *World Crisis and American Responsibility*, p. 76.

53. Franks, *American Soldier*, p. 203.

54. Ibid., p. 341. Emphasis in the original.

Conclusion: The Limits of Power

1. David Carr, "Someone Give Geffen a Day Job," *New York Times*, February 26, 2007.

2. Niebuhr, *World Crisis and American Responsibility*, p. 41.

3. Ibid.

4. "President's Remarks at National Day of Prayer and Remembrance," September 14, 2001.

5. For a more detailed and insightful examination of this alternative strategy, see Ian Shapiro, *Containment: Rebuilding a Strategy against Global Terror* (Princeton, N.J., 2007).

6. "U.S. Nuclear Weapon Enduring Stockpile," August 31, 2007, http://nuclearweaponarchive.org/Usa/Weapons/Wpngall.html, accessed January 31, 2008.

7. Niebuhr, *Irony of American History*, p. 57.

8. Niebuhr, *World Crisis and American Responsibility*, p. 85.

9. Niebuhr, *Moral Man and Immoral Society*, p. 83.

10. Niebuhr, *Beyond Tragedy*, p. 224.

Acknowledgments

The publication of this book coincides with the tenth anniversary of my service with Boston University. Wonderful students and stimulating colleagues have made teaching at BU a life-transforming experience. I wish to acknowledge in particular the generosity and support of my departmental chairs, Charles Dellheim and Erik Goldstein.

In completing this project, I have accrued many other debts. I want to thank Sara Bershtel of Metropolitan Books for her trust and confidence. My editor Tom Englehardt has been nothing short of terrific—a font of good ideas, large and small. I drew not only on the ideas but on the energy and feistiness that Tom unfailingly exudes. Vicki Haire did an outstanding job of copyediting the manuscript.

I thank my old friends Bill Arkin, Chris Gray, Lawrence Kaplan, and David Warsh for allowing me to tap their expertise. I am also grateful for the timely contributions of several research assistants: Joe Brown, Zack Matusheski, and above all the estimable Conor Savoy. Good job, fellows.

I probably shouldn't say this, but I have ceased to think of John Wright as my agent. He has become a dear friend, a source of wisdom and counsel and, this time around, of consolation as well.

My darling Nancy has been my partner through what now qualifies as a long journey. This past year has not been an easy one. Through it all, she has demonstrated courage, grace, and dignity. She remains a source of constant inspiration.

I have dedicated this book to our son, who on May 13, 2007, was killed in action in Iraq, one of some four thousand American soldiers to have lost their lives in that war. His memory remains sacred to his friends and to all the members of his family. His mother and his father will mourn his passing until the last day.

Index

About the Author

ANDREW J. BACEVICH is a professor of history and international relations at Boston University. He is the author of *The New American Militarism*, among other books. His writing has appeared in *Foreign Affairs*, *The Atlantic Monthly*, *The Nation*, *The New York Times*, *The Washington Post*, and *The Wall Street Journal*. He is the recipient of a Lannan award and a member of the Council on Foreign Relations.

The American Empire Project

In an era of unprecedented military strength, leaders of the United States, the global hyperpower, have increasingly embraced imperial ambitions. How did this significant shift in purpose and policy come about? And what lies down the road?

The American Empire Project is a response to the changes that have occurred in America's strategic thinking as well as in its military and economic posture. Empire, long considered an offense against America's democratic heritage, now threatens to define the relationship between our country and the rest of the world. The American Empire Project publishes books that question this development, examine the origins of U.S. imperial aspirations, analyze their ramifications at home and abroad, and discuss alternatives to this dangerous trend.

The project was conceived by Tom Engelhardt and Steve

Fraser, editors who are themselves historians and writers. Published by Metropolitan Books, an imprint of Henry Holt and Company, its titles include *Hegemony or Survival* by Noam Chomsky, *The Sorrows of Empire* by Chalmers Johnson, *Crusade* by James Carroll, *How to Succeed at Globalization* by El Fisgón, *Blood and Oil* by Michael Klare, *Dilemmas of Domination* by Walden Bello, *War Powers* by Peter Irons, *Devil's Game* by Robert Dreyfuss, *In the Name of Democracy*, edited by Jeremy Brecher, Jill Cutler, and Brendan Smith, *Imperial Ambitions* by Noam Chomsky, *A Question of Torture* by Alfred McCoy, *Failed States* by Noam Chomsky, and *Empire's Workshop* by Greg Grandin.

For more information about the American Empire Project and for a list of forthcoming titles, please visit www .americanempireproject.com.